Winning with the Schliemann

Maxwell Macmillan Chess Openings

Executive Editor: PAUL LAMFORD
Technical Editor: JIMMY ADAMS
Russian Series Editor: KEN NEAT

Some other books in this series:

ADORJAN, A. & HORVATH, T.
Sicilian: Sveshnikov Variation

ASSIAC & O'CONNELL, K.
Opening Preparation

BASMAN, M.
Play the St. George
The Killer Grob

CAFFERTY, B. & HOOPER, D.
A Complete Defence to 1 e4

GLIGORIC, S.
Play the Nimzo-Indian Defence

KEENE, R.D.
The Evolution of Chess Opening Theory

KOVACS, L.M.
Sicilian: Poisoned Pawn Variation

MAROVIC, D.
Play the King's Indian Defence
Play the Queen's Gambit

NEISHTADT, I.
Play the Catalan
   Volume 1 – Open Variation
   Volume 2 – Closed Variation

PRZEWOZNIK, J. & PEIN, M.
The Blumenfeld Gambit

SHAMKOVICH, L. & SCHILLER, E.
Play the Tarrasch

SUETIN, A.S.
Modern Chess Opening Theory

TAULBUT, S.
Play the Bogo-Indian

VARNUSZ, E.
Play the Caro-Kann
Play Anti-Indian Systems

WATSON, J.L.
Play the French

A full catalogue is available from:
Maxwell Macmillan Chess, London Road, Wheatley, Oxford, OX9 1YR.

Winning with the Schliemann

by
Mikhail Tseitlin
International Grandmaster

MAXWELL MACMILLAN CHESS

MAXWELL MACMILLAN INTERNATIONAL PUBLISHING GROUP

EUROPE/
MIDDLE EAST/AFRICA

Maxwell Macmillan International,
Nuffield Building, Hollow Way, Cowley,
Oxford OX4 2YH, England
Tel: (0865) 748754   Fax: (0865) 748808

USA

Macmillan Publishing Company,
866 Third Avenue, New York, NY 10022
Tel: (212) 702-2000   Fax: (212) 605-9341

CANADA

1200 Eglinton Avenue East,
Suite 200, Don Mills, Ontario M3C 3N1, Canada
Tel: (416) 449-6030   Fax: (416) 449-0068

AUSTRALIA/
NEW ZEALAND

Lakes Business Park, Building A1,
2 Lord Street, Botany, NSW 2019, Australia
Tel: (02) 316-9444   Fax: (02) 316-9485

ASIA/PACIFIC
(Except Japan)

72 Hillview Avenue, #03-00 Tacam House, Singapore 2
Tel: (65) 769-6000   Fax: (65) 769-3731

LATIN AMERICA

28100 US Highway 19 North,
Suite 200, Clearwater, FL 34621, USA
Tel: (813) 725-4033   Fax: (813) 725-2185

JAPAN

Misuzu S Building 2F, 2-42-14 Matsubara Setagaya-k
Tokyo 156, Japan
Tel: (81) 3-5300-1618   Fax: (81) 3-5300-1615

First Edition 1991

Library of Congress Cataloging-in-Publication Data

Tseitlin, Mikhail.
Winning with the Schliemann /
by Mikhail Tseitlin. — 1st ed.
p.   cm.   — (Maxwell Macmillan chess openings)
Includes index.
1. Chess — Openings.   I. Title.   II. Series.
GV1450.2.T74   1991
794.1'22—dc20   91-20072

British Library Cataloguing in Publication Data

Tseitlin, Mikhail
Winning with the schliemann.
I. Title
794.12

ISBN 1 85744 017 X

Cover by Pintail Design
Printed in Great Britain by BPCC Wheatons Ltd, Exeter

Contents

Symbols

+	Check
!	Good move
!!	Excellent move
?	Bad move
??	Blunder
!?	Interesting move
?!	Dubious move
(!)	Best move in difficult circumstances
±	Small advantage for White
∓	Small advantage for Black
±	Clear advantage for White
∓	Clear advantage for Black
+-	Winning advantage for White
-+	Winning advantage for Black
1 : 0	White wins
0 : 1	Black wins
½ : ½	Draw
=	The position is equal
∞	The position is unclear
⧝	With counterplay
↑	With attack
△	With the idea of
□	Only move
Ch.	Championship
Ol.	Olympiad

The Jaenisch Gambit

Introduction

In 1847, in the French magazine *Le Palamède* a well known Russian chess-player, Karl Andreyevich Jaenisch published the first analysis of the gambit in the Spanish game that occurs after: 1 e4 e5 2 ♘f3 ♘c6 3 ♗b5 f5.

Here he wrote: "This countergambit has not been mentioned by any author and has not been played anywhere. It is a very interesting possibility, and in many variations Black obtains excellent counterchances."

Since then, this gambit has been rightfully known as the Jaenisch Gambit. It should be noted that in many places the gambit is connected with the name of the German chess-player A. Schliemann. This is incorrect, as Schliemann used the move ... f5 only in conjunction with 3 ... ♗c5 4 0-0.

The newly born gambit did not experience an immediate success. Indeed, the first blow to its credibility was dealt by the author himself! In 1850, in the magazine *Deutsche Schachzeitung* Jaenisch wrote that White can successfully fight for the initiative with 4 ♕e2. Further analyses by I. Bannet (1899) and E. Dyckhoff (1902) also claimed easy advantages for White against the gambit and it seemed as though this method of defence would disappear from view.

However, the beginning of the twentieth century witnessed a revival of interest in Jaenisch's Gambit. It was analysed by the World Champion of the time, Emanuel Lasker and also by other leading players including K. Bardeleben, F. Duz-Hotimirsky, R. Spielmann and especially F. Marshall, who even risked the gambit in some games in his match against Capablanca (New York, 1909), and with some success.

This revival was not necessarily connected with special innovations from the Black point of view, but more because the Spanish game had begun to predominate in open games. For a long time adherents of 1 ... e5 were unable to find an effective antidote against the 'Spanish torture' and the quest for counterplay was leading to research in all directions.

However, Jaenisch's Gambit only really began to be played consistently in tournament practice around thirty years ago, and even today there exists a certain scepticism about the overall viability of the gambit.

The authors have collated and researched a vast amount of theoretical and practical material in the present monograph. If, as a result, the gambit is demonstrated as a perfectly feasible counter to the 'Spanish torture', then this effort will have been worth while.

Mikhail Tseitlin,
E. Glaskov.

1) 4 exf5 and others

1	e4	e5
2	♘f3	♘c6
3	♗b5	f5

4   exf5

This simple capture doesn't present Black with any difficulties and so is not often seen. However, it should be noted that, by playing like this, White can force a draw at will.

In the event of **4 0-0**, Black gets the advantage after 4 ... fxe4 5 ♗xc6 dxc6 6 ♘xe5 ♕d4 7 ♘g4 (7 ♕h5+ g6 8 ♘xg6 hxg6) 7 ... h5 8 ♘e3 ♘f6 as in Amateur – van Vliet, London 1899

Interesting complications can arise after **4 ♗xc6**. The game Schroder – Nimzovitch, Berlin 1903 continued 4 ... bxc6 5 ♘xe5 ♕e7 6 ♕h5+ g6 7 ♘xg6 hxg6!? (Youthful fervour! Nimzovitch was only sixteen) 8 ♕xh8 ♕xe4+ 9 ♔f1? (necessary was 9 ♔d1 ♕xg2 10 ♖e1+ ♔f7 11 ♕e5 ♕xf2 with equality) 9 ... ♕xc2! 10 ♘c3 No better is 10 ♕e5+ ♔f7 11 ♕e1 in view of 11 ... ♗a6+ 12 d3 ♗xd3+ 13 ♔g1 ♖e8) 10 ... ♕d3+! 11 ♔g1 ♔f7 12 h3 ♗a6 13 ♔h2 ♕d6+ 14 g3 ♘f6! and Black won.

Instead of 5 ♘xe5 correct is 5 exf5! and after 5 ... e4 6 ♕e2 ♕e7 7 ♘d4 ♕e5! 8 ♘f3 ♕e7! leads to repetition, as 8 ... ♕xf5 9 d3 ♘f6 10 ♘bd2 d5 11 ♘d4 ♕g6 12 0-0 is in White's favour. Alternatively 7 ... ♘f6 leads to 8 0-0! c5 (or 8 ... ♕e5 9 ♘f3 ♕e7 10 ♖e1) 9 ♘b5! d5 10 f3! with a clear advantage.

In response to the capture on c6 on move 4, Black usually responds 4 ... dxc6

with the following possibilities:

a) **5 exf5** e4 6 ♕e2 ♕e7 leads to the main continuation.

b) **5 ♕e2** fxe4 6 ♕xe4 will be examined in the second chapter.

c) **5 ♘xe5** ♕d4 6 ♘f3 (after 6 ♕h5+? g6 7 ♘xg6 hxg6 8 ♕xg6+ ♔d8 9 d3 ♘e7 White has no compensation for the piece, as Jaenisch showed) 6 ... ♕xe4+ 7 ♕e2 ♗d6 with splendid play for Black.

d) **5 ♘c3** ♘f6 6 ♕e2 fxe4 7 ♘xe4 ♗g4 8 h3 ♗h5

(simpler is 8 ... ♗xf3 9 ♕xf3 ♕d5 with full equality). Here the game Nicevsky – Velimirovic, Yugoslavia 1981 continued 9 d3 ♕d5 10 g4 (if 10 0-0 then 10 ... ♗xf3! 11 ♕xf3 0-0-0) 10 ... ♗f7 11 ♘c3 ♗b4 12 ♕xe5+ ♔d7! 13 ♕xd5+ ♗xd5 14 ♔e2 ♘xc3 15 bxc3 ♖hf8 16 c4 ♖ae8+ 17 ♗e3 ♗xf3+ 18 ♔xf3, and after 18 ... ♘d5+ 19 ♔e2 ♘f4+ 20 ♔d2 ♘g2 21 ♖af1 ♖f3 chances were completely equal. In the game Ryabchenok – Mik. Tseitlin, Kuibishev 1981, White tried 9 ♘g3 but after 9 ♘g3 ♗xf3 10 ♕xf3 ♕d5 11 ♔e2 e4 12 ♕f5 ♗d6 13 ♕xd5 cxd5 14 ♘f5 0-0-0 15 d4 exd3+ 16 ♔xd3 ♘e4 17 ♗e3 ♗c5 18 f3 ♘f2+ Black stood better.

Now we return to the main variation after

4   exf5

4   ...   e4

The recommendation of the old handbooks, **4 ... d6 5 d4 e4** is weak on account of 6 ♘g5 ♗xf5 7 f3.

The best response to **4 ... ♗c5** is **5 ♕e2!** The alternative 5 ♗xc6 dxc6 6 ♘xe5 ♗xf5 gives Black a good chance to develop an initiative, e.g. 7 0-0 7 ... ♘f6 8 ♖e1 0-0 9 c3 ♗d3 10 ♕b3+ ♔h8 11 ♘f7+ ♖xf7 12 ♕xf7 ♘g4! with a tremendous attack, Kade - Schliemann, Berlin 1867. Or 7 ♕h5+ g6 8 ♘xg6 hxg6! 9 ♕xh8 ♕e7+ 10 ♔d1 (10 ♔f1 doesn't help after 10 ... ♗xc2 11 ♕xg8+ ♔d7 12 ♕c4 ♖e8) 10 ... ♗xf2! 11 ♕xg8+ ♔d7 12 ♕c4 ♖e8 0 : 1 Shletser - Tchigorin, Petersburg 1878.

5 ♕e2

The variation **5 ♗xc6 dxc6 6 ♘e5** (better 6 ♕e2 leading to the main continuation) 6 ... ♗xf5 is favourable for Black, e.g 7 ♕h5+ g6 8 ♘xg6 ♗xg6 9 ♕e5+ ♕e7 10 ♕xh8 ♘f6 and the White queen is trapped, Rindin - Glazkov, Tula 1954, or 7 0-0 ♕d4 8 ♘g4 ♗xf5 9 ♘e3 ♗g6 10 ♘c3 0-0-0 11 ♘e2 ♕e5 12 ♘c4 ♕f5∓ Zarubin - Nesterenko, Moscow 1972.

Also unsatisfactory is **5**

♘g1 ♘f6 6 ♘e2 d5 7 ♘g3 h5 8 c4 h4 9 ♘e2 ♗xf5 with excellent play for Black, Berezhnoi - Nikonov, USSR 1971.

5 ... ♕e7
6 ♗xc6 dxc6

After 6 ... bxc6 a position arises which was considered in the note to White's fourth.

7 ♘d4 ♕e5

The recommendation of Jaenisch, 7 ... c5 is mistaken in view of 8 ♘e6! ♘f6 9 ♘c3 ♗xe6 10 fxe6 ♕xe6 11 d3 and Black loses a pawn.

8 ♘e6

The strongest move for White is **8 ♘f3!** ♕e7 (but not 8 ... ♕xf5 because of 9 d3) leading to a repetition of moves.

8 ♘b3 is unsatisfactory after 8 ... ♗d6 9 f3 (9 ♘a3 ♗xa3 10 bxa3 ♗xf5 11 ♖b1 ♘f6 is good for Black) 9 ... exf3 10 ♕xe5+ ♗xe5 11 0-0 ♘e7.

8 ...   ♗xe6
9 fxe6   ♗d6

9 ... ♕xe6? 10 d3!
10 ♘c3   ♘f6
11 b3   0-0-0
12 ♗b2

12 h3 ♘d5 13 ♗b2 e3! Borchardt - Grabczewski, Poland 1977.

Tournament   practice
demonstrates   that   Black

has the initiative in this
position, e.g.

12 ... ♖de8 13 0-0-0 ♖xe6
14 ♖de1 ♕f5 15 ♔b1 ♖he8
and Black's chances are
preferable, Cuellar – Bisguier, Bogota 1958.

12 ... ♖he8 13 0-0-0 ♖xe6
14 f3 exf3 15 ♕xf3 ♕f4 16
♖hf1 ♕xf3 17 ♖xf3 ♗xh2 and
Black has won a pawn
Bokuchava – Mik. Tseitlin,
Sukhumi 1974.

2) 4 ♕e2

1	e4	e5
2	♘f3	♘c6
3	♗b5	f5
4	♕e2	

K. Jaenisch considered this continuation to be the best (Deutsche Schachzeitung, 1850), but in reality it can only be worse for White.

4 ... fxe4

The usual response. According to Jaenisch, also possible is **4 ... ♘d4 5 ♘xd4 exd4 6 exf5+ ♕e7=** as White cannot hold the pawn. In the game Bogdanovic - Kurajica, Yugoslavia 1985, the original move **4 ... ♕e7!** led to complications following **5 d3 ♕b4+ 6 ♘c3 ♘d4 7 ♘xd4 exd4 8 exf5+ ♔d8 9 a3 ♕a5 10 ♗g5+.**

After the text move there are two possibilities:

A) 5 ♗xc6
B) 5 ♕xe4

A)

5	♗xc6	dxc6
6	♕xe4	

6 ...   ♗d6

Here attention should be given to the sacrifice **6 ... ♘f6!?** 7 ♕xe5+ (7 ♕e2 ♗d6 leads to the main continuation) 7 ... ♗e7. The game Gumruksnoglu – Ciocaltea, Balkaniada 1980 went 8 d4 0-0 9 ♕e2 ♗g4! 10 ♕c4+ ♘d5 11 ♘e5 ♗e6 12 ♗e3 (if 12 ♕e2 ♗g5!) 12 ... ♗g5, and after 13 ♘f3 (13 ♕e2 ♗xe3 14 fxe3 ♕h4+ 15 g3 ♕e4) 13 ... ♗xe3 14 fxe3 ♕e7 15 ♕e2 ♗g4 Black was fine.

In the game Agapov – Kislov, Leningrad 1981, White took a different route: 8 ♘c3 0-0 9 ♕e2 ♘d5 (9 ... ♗g4 10 ♕c4+ ♔h8 11 ♘e5 ♗h5 12 0-0 ♕d6 13 d4 ♘g4 14 ♘xg4 ♗xg4=) 10 ♘xd5, but after 10 ... ♕xd5!? 11 ♕xe7 ♗g4 12 0-0 ♗xf3 13 ♖e1 ♗xg2 14 ♕e6+ ♕xe6 15 ♖xe6 ♗d5 Black was doing very well.

7 ♘xe5

7 d3 ♘f6 8 ♕e2 0-0 9 ♗g5 ♕e8 10 ♗xf6 gxf6 11 ♘bd2 ♔h8 12 0-0-0 ♕f7∓ Petrushin – Lutikov, RSFSR 1986. Capturing the pawn does not advance White's cause.

7 ...   ♘f6
8 ♕e2   0-0
9 d4

9 ♕c4+? ♘d5 10 d4 ♕h4∓

9 ...   ♖e8

9 ... ♕e8!? 10 f4 (10 0-0 is best met by 10 ... c5 11 c3 cxd4 12 cxd4 c5 developing great activity for the pawn, e.g 13 ♖e1 cxd4 14 ♕c4+ ♗e6 15 ♕xd4 ♖d8) 10 ... c5 11 dxc5 ♗xe5 12 fxe5 (12 ♕xe5 ♕g6!) 12 ... ♘g4 13 ♗d2 ♖f2 14 ♕c4+ ♗e6 15 ♕c3 ♕c6 16 ♔d1 ♕xg2∓ Doroshkevich – Bergin, Moscow 1963.

10 0-0

The attempt to strengthen the position of the knight, **10 f4** doesn't advance White's cause, e.g. 10 ... c5 11 ♗e3 ♘g4 12 c3 cxd4 13 cxd4 c5 14 0-0 ♘xe3 15 ♕xe3 ♕b6∓ (Chigorin).

10 ♗e3 ♗xe5 11 dxe5 ♖xe5 12 ♘d2 ♗g4 13 ♕c4+ ♕d5 14 0-0 ♖ae8 is also better for Black, Kozlov – Mik. Tseitlin, Moscow 1976.

10 ...   ♗xe5
11 dxe5   ♕d4
12 ♖d1

Tchigorin here ends his analysis with **12 ... ♕xe5** which gives Black full equality. However, in Survillo – Glazkov, Moscow 1978, Black decided to fight for more with **12 ... ♖xe5!** 13 ♖xd4 ♖xe2 14 ♖d8+ ♔f7 15 ♗d2 ♘e4 16 f3! ♗h3!, but after 17 ♖xa8 ♖xg2+ 18 ♔f1 ♖xh2+ 19 ♔e1 ♘xd2 the chances were equal. Better would have been 15 ... ♔e7! 16 ♖h8 b6 17 f3 c5 and White has problems with his development.

B

| 5 | ♕xe4 | ♘f6 |
| 6 | ♕e2 | |

6 ... ♗d6!
This is an original idea of V. Zak. Much inferior is 6 ... e4 7 d3 d5 8 dxe4 dxe4 in view of 9 ♘e5! ♗d7 (9 ... ♕d5 10 ♗xc6+ bxc6 11 ♘c4) 10 ♗xc6 ♗xc6 11 ♘xc6 bxc6

12 ♘c3 ♗b4 13 ♗d2.
6 ... d6 was tried in Marco – Bernstein, Stockholm 1906, but after 7 d4 e4 8 d5 ♘xd5 9 ♘d4 ♘de7 10 ♕xe4 ♗d7 Black had a cramped position, but 9 ... ♘db4! gives Black satisfactory play.

7 d4
7 ♗c4 ♗e7 (7 ... ♕e7!? is interesting, e.g. 8 0-0 e4 9 ♘g5 ♗xh2+) 8 d4 (8 ♘xe5 ♘xe5 9 ♕xe5 d5 and 10 ... 0-0 grants Black a dangerous initiative for the pawn) 8 ... e4 9 ♘e5 ♘xd4 10 ♕d1 ♘e6 and White remains a pawn behind, Okhtman – Shekhtman, Leningrad 1964.

| 7 | ... | e4 |
| 8 | ♘g5 | ♕e7 |

8 ... ♘xd4? is a blunder on account of 9 ♕c4! and Black loses, but deserving of attention is 8 ... 0-0!?

| 9 | c3 | h6 |
| 10 | ♘h3 | g5 |

In practice, Black has had the better chances in this position, as the following examples show:

a) 11 ♘d2 b6 12 ♘c4 ♗b7 13 ♘xd6+ ♕xd6 14 f4 g4 15 ♘f2 0-0-0 Konstantinov - Zak, Leningrad 1959.

b) 11 0-0 0-0 12 f3 (better is 12 ♗e3 and then ♘d2) 12 ... exf3 13 ♕c4+ (13 ♕xe7 ♘xe7 14 gxf3∓) 13 ... ♔g7 14 ♖xf3 ♘g4 15 ♖xf8 ♕xf8 16 g3 ♘xh2! with a dangerous attack, Bangiev - Agzamov, Tashkent 1964.

c) 11 ♘xg5 hxg5 12 ♗xg5 e3! 13 f4 b6 14 ♘a3 ♗xa3 15 bxa3 ♗b7 16 0-0 0-0-0 17 ♖f3 ♖de8 18 ♖e1 ♕f7 19 ♗c4 ♘d5∓ Vitolinsh - Lanka, Riga 1978.

3) 4 d3

1	e4	e5
2	♘f3	♘c6
3	♗b5	f5
4	d3	

This continuation is better than the ones previously examined, but it cannot be claimed to be a refutation of Jaenisch's Gambit. In fact White must be careful not to play too passively, when Black can develop a swift kingside attack, in the manner of a King's Gambit Declined with colours reversed. If the black bishop comes to c5, as it does in the modern variation, there is already a certain amount of pressure against the f2 square. This can be augmented by maneouvres such as ♕d8 – e8 – g6 (or h5), ♘f6 – h5 – f4 or even ♖f8 – f6 – g6 (or h6). Many unsuspecting Whites have found themselves chopped up on the kingside in short order in this line.

Now Black has a choice between an immediate exchange in the centre or preparation for complex play –

A) 4 ... fxe4
B) 4 ... ♘f6

A

4	...	fxe4
5	dxe4	♘f6

This move solves the

problem of the development of the king's bishop (see A1 below). Also possible is **5 ... d6**, which after 6 0-0 ♘f6 leads to A2. Instead of 6 0-0 practice has also witnessed:

a) **6 ♗xc6+** bxc6 7 0-0 ♗e7 8 ♕d3 ♗f6! is comfortable for Black, Fiebig – Nyholm, Hamburg 1910.

b) **6 ♗g5** ♗e7 7 ♗xe7 ♘gxe7 8 ♗c4 ♘g6 9 c3 ♕f6 10 ♘bd2 ♗d7 11 ♕c2 ♘f4 Ilyin-Zhenevsky – Nyholm, Leningrad 1926.

c) **6 c4** ♘f6 7 ♘c3 ♗g4 8 ♕d3 ♗e7 9 ♘d5 0-0 10 ♘xe7+ ♕xe7 11 ♗a4 ♘d7∓ Crepeaux – Lazard, Paris 1930.

d) **6 ♘c3** ♘f6?! (6 ... ♗g4 7 ♘d5 ♘f6 8 ♗g5 ♗e7 9 ♘xe7 ♕xe7 10 h3 ♗e6 11 ♕e2 h6 12 ♗xf6 ♕xf6 13 0-0 0-0-0 leads to equality, Bradvarevic – Maric, Sombor 1957, and is preferable to the text) 7 ♗g5 ♗e7 8 ♗xf6 ♗xf6 9 ♕d5 ♗d7 10 0-0-0 ♕e7 11 ♖he1 0-0-0 12 ♕c4! g5 13 ♘d5 ♕g7 14 ♖e3! and White stood well, Farah – Merlo, Villa Gesela 1968. An alternative approach was seen in Forgacs – Hebak, Prague 1973 – 8 ♗c4 ♗g4 (8 ... ♘a5 9 ♕e2 ♗g4 10

0-0-0 ♕c8 11 h3 ♘xc4 12 hxg4! ♘b6 13 ♗xf6 ♗xf6 14 g5 ♗e7 15 g6±) 9 ♕d3 ♕d7 10 0-0-0 0-0-0 (better is 10 ... a6!?) and after 11 ♗e3 ♗e6 12 ♘d5 ♘g4 13 ♗b5!±.

6 0-0

This is the most common continuation, but the other possibilities are important:

a) **6 ♘c3** ♗b4! 7 ♕d3 d6 8 ♗d2 ♗xc3 9 ♗xc3 0-0 (9 ... ♗d7 10 0-0-0 ♕e7 11 ♕e3 0-0 12 h3 ♔h8 13 ♗c4 a5 14 ♔b1 ♗e6 with good play for Black, Incutto – Spassky, Mar del Plata 1960) 10 0-0-0 ♕e8 11 h3 a6 12 ♗c4+ ♗e6 13 ♖he1 ♗xc4 14 ♕xc4+ ♔h8 15 ♕e2 ♘d7 16 ♔b1 b5 with an active position, Nezhmetdinov – Bronstein, Tbilisi 1959.

b) **6 ♗xc6** bxc6 7 ♕e2 ♗d6 8 ♘bd2 0-0 9 h3 ♘h5 10 ♘c4 ♕f6 11 ♗g5 ♕g6 12 g4 ♘f4 13 ♗xf4 ♖xf4∓ Chistiakov – Ravinsky, Moscow 1961. In the correspondence game Tiller – Boey 1972/75, White played the risky 7 ♘xe5 ♕e7 8 ♗f4 (8 ♘f3 ♕xe4+ 9 ♗e3 ♗a6) a decision he was to regret after 8 ... g5! 9 ♗g3 d6 10 ♘d3 ♕xe4+ 11 ♔d2 ♕f5 12 ♘c3 ♗h6 13 ♕e2+ ♔f7 14 f3 (14 ♔c1 g4+ 15 ♔b1 ♖e8, or 14 ♘d1 g4+ 15 ♘e3 ♖e8 16 ♖hf1 ♕e4 with advantage to Black in both cases) 14 ... g4+ 15 f4 c5 16 ♖ae1 ♖e8 17 ♕f2 ♗b7 18 ♖xe8 ♖xe8 19 ♖e1 ♖xe1 20 ♕xe1∓.

c) **6 ♗c4 ♗c5 7 0-0 d6**, reaching a position from the King's Gambit Declined with colours reversed. Now after 8 ♘c3 ♘a5 9 ♗b3 ♘xb3 10 axb3 a6! or 8 c3 ♕e7! 9 b4 ♗b6 10 ♘bd2 a5 11 b5 ♘d8 12 ♗a3 ♗g4 13 ♕c2 ♘d7! 14 ♔h1 ♖f8 15 ♗e2 ♗e6 16 ♖ad1 g5! Black has the initiative.

d) **6 ♗g5 ♗c5! 7 ♘c3 d6 8 ♕d3** (8 0-0 leads to the main continuation) 8 ... ♗b4 9 0-0-0 ♗xc3 10 ♕xc3 ♗d7 11 ♘d2 ♘d4 12 ♗xd7+ ♕xd7= Martinovic – Velimirovic, Arandzelovac 1980. Interesting complications can arise from the alternative 8 ♗xf6 ♕xf6 9 ♘d5 ♕d8

(worthy of serious attention is 9 ... ♕g6!? 10 0-0 0-0 11 ♘xc7 ♗h3 12 ♘h4 ♕g5 13 ♘xa8 ♕xh4 14 gxh3 ♕xh3 with a strong attack) 10 b4 (10 0-0 0-0 and with ... ♗g4 coming, Black is fine) 10 ... ♗b6 11 a4 a6 12 ♘xb6 cxb6 13 ♗c4 ♘xb4 14 ♕d2 ♘c6 15 ♘g5 (Raina – Yudasin, Budapest 1982) and now according to Yudasin, either 15 ... ♕f6 16 ♘f7 ♖f8 17 ♘xd6+ ♔e7 18 ♖d1 ♘d4 or 15 ... ♖f8 16 ♘xh7 ♖f4 17 0-0 ♕h4 18 g3 ♕xh7 leave Black with the better prospects.

e) **6 ♕d3 ♗b4+** (6 ... ♗c5 7 ♘c3 d6 8 ♗g5 was examined in the previous line) 7 c3 ♗c5 8 0-0 (8 ♗xc6 bxc6 9 ♘xe5 ♕e7 10 f4 ♗b7 11 ♘d2 d6 12 ♘ef3 0-0 intending ♖ae8, with sufficient compensation for the pawn) 8 ... d6 9 a4 a6 10 ♗c4 (10 ♗xc6+ bxc6 11 ♕c4 ♕d7) 10 ... ♕e7 11 ♘bd2 ♗e6 12 b4 ♗a7=, Kindermann – Inkiov, Berlin 1986.

f) **6 ♕e2 ♗c5 7 ♗xc6** (7 c3 d6 8 0-0 leads to the main continuation, and if 8 ♘bd2 possible are 8 ... a5 or 8 ... a6) 7 ... bxc6 8 ♘xe5 ♕e7 9 ♘d3 ♗a6 10 ♗g5 ♘d4 11 ♘c3 ♗xc3+ 12 bxc3 ♕xe4 13 ♗xf6 ♕xe2+= Rozentalis – Glek,

Tallinn 1986. An alternative to 6 ... ♗c5 is 6 ... ♗b4+ 7 c3 ♗c5. Two examples from this position are: 8 ♘bd2 ♕e7 9 ♘c4 d6 10 b4 ♗b6 11 a4 a6 12 ♘xb6 cxb6 13 ♗c4= Ermenkov - Mik. Tseitlin, Pamporovo 1977 and 8 0-0 d6 9 a4 a6 10 ♗xc6+ bxc6 11 a5 ♗e6 12 b4 ♗a7 13 ♗e3 ♗xe3 14 ♕xe3 0-0= Short - Hecht, England 1982.

Returning to 6 0-0.

Now Black can choose between two continuations:

A1) The modern 6 ... ♗c5.
A2) The classical 6 ... d6.

A1

> **6 ... ♗c5**

This active posting for the bishop is currently the most popular choice.

7   ♘c3

The usual response, but White has a number of alternative possibilities:

a) 7 ♕e2 d6 8 c3 0-0 9 a4 (9 ♘bd2 ♗g4!? (9 ... ♔h8!? is possible) 10 ♗xc6 bxc6 11 ♕c4+ ♔h8 12 ♘xe5 ♕e8 and Black has an excellent position, Yusto - Lanni, Lucerne 1982. The continuation was 13 ♘ef3 ♕h5 14 ♕d3 ♘d7 15 h3 ♗e6 16 ♘d4 ♘e5 17 ♕g3 ♗c8! 18 ♘2f3 ♗a6 19 ♘e6 ♘xf3+ 20 gxf3 ♖f7∓) 9 ... a5 10 ♘bd2 ♔h8 11 ♘b3 ♗b6 12 ♗e3 ♗xe3 13 ♕xe3 ♕e8 14 ♘bd2 ♘h5 and Black has obtained the initiative, Short - Nunn, Marbella 1982.

In Martin - Inkiov, Gausdal 1989, instead of 8 c3, 8 ♕c4 was tried with the continuation 8 ... ♕e7 9 ♘c3 (9 b4 ♗e6 10 ♕c3 ♘xe4!? 11 ♕d3 ♘xf2 with strong counterplay) 9 ... ♗d7 10 ♘d5 (10 ♗g5 a6!) 10 ... ♘xd5 11 exd5 ♘d4 12 ♗xd7+ ♕xd7 13 ♘xd4 ♗xd4=. Martin mentions 13 ♘xe5!? ♕f5! 14 b4 b5 15 ♕d3, but after 15 ... ♕xd3! 16 ♘xd3 (16 cxd3 ♘e2+ 17 ♔h1 ♗d4) 16 ... ♘e2+ 17 ♔h1 ♗d4 18 ♖b1 ♘c3 Black has the better prospects.

b) **7 ♘bd2** ♕e7 (7 ... 0-0 8 c3 d6 9 ♕e2 leads to a position from the preceding example) 8 c3 a6 9 ♗c4 d6 10 b4 ♗a7 11 a4 ♘d8∓ Kremenetsky - Mik. Tseitlin, Moscow 1976.

c) **7 ♕d3** d6 8 ♘bd2 (8 a4 a6!) 8 ... ♕e7 9 ♘c4 (9 c3 a6!) 9 ... 0-0 10 ♗e3 ♗xe3 11 ♘xe3 ♔h8 12 c4 ♘h5 13 c5?! Urzica - Hecht, Romania 1980. Better than White's 13th is 13 ♘d5 ♕d8. Now Black could have got the advantage with 13 ... ♖xf3! 14 ♗xc6 ♖xe3! It should also be noted that 8 ... a6 is possible: 9 ♗c4 ♘a5 10 ♖e1 ♕e7; 9 ♗xc6+ bxc6 10 ♘b3 ♗b6 11 ♗e3 a5 or 9 ♗a4 ♕e7 10 c3 b5 11 ♗b3 ♘d8 12 ♖e1 ♗e6 with equal play in all cases.

d) **7 ♗xc6** bxc6 8 ♘xe5 0-0. This variation is of great importance for the tactical justification of 6 ... ♗c5. Let's examine White's possibilities:

di) **9 ♗g5** ♕e8 10 ♗xf6 ♖xf6 11 ♘d3 ♗d4 12 c3 (Spassky attempted to improve over this with 12 ♘d2 but could make little impression on the black position after 12 ... d6 13 ♕e2 ♕g6 14 ♔h1 ♗a6 15 ♖ab1 ♖af8 16 f3 ♕g5 17 ♖fd1 ½-½ Spassky - Antunes, Thessaloniki ol 1988. Black's bishops and active position provide ample compensation for the pawn) 12 ... ♗b6 13 ♘d2 ♗a6 14 c4 d5 15 e5 ♖f8 16 ♕e2 ♕g6 and Black has excellent counterplay for the pawn. Wolff - Kolev, Kiljava 1984.

dii) **9 ♘c3** ♗a6! 10 ♘d3 ♕e7 and now: if 11 e5 then 11 ... ♘d5; if 11 ♗g5 ♗d4 and finally after 11 ♖e1 Black plays 11 ... ♗xd3 12 cxd3

♗xf2+ 13 ♔xf2 ♘g4+ 14 ♔g1 ♕h4 15 h3 ♕g3!!–+.

diii) **9 ♕e2 ♕e7** 10 ♘d3 ♗a6 11 ♘c3 ♗d4 12 ♖e1 ♖ae8 13 e5 ♗xd3 (good is 13 ... ♕f7) 14 ♕xd3 and after 14 ... ♗xe5 15 ♘f4 ♘g4 16 ♗xe5 ♘xe5 Black wins a pawn with the better position, Schneider – Greenfeld, Beersheva 1980. Maia de Alzate – Butskinlhom, Lucerne 1982 saw instead 10 ♕c4+ ♔h8 11 ♘d3 ♗b6 (11 ... ♘xe4 is possible) 12 e5 ♘d5 13 ♘c3 ♗b7 14 ♘e4 ♖f5 15 ♘g3 ♖f7 16 ♕g4 ♖af8 17 ♗g5 ♕e6 with a double-edged position where Black has sufficient compensation for the pawn.

Returning to the main continuation:

7   ...   d6
Risky is **7 ... 0-0?!** in view of 8 ♘g5! ♔h8 9 ♗c4 ♕e8 10 ♘d5 ♘b6 11 ♗e3 ♕g6 12 h4 h6 13 ♘xf6 ♖xf6 14 ♕d5 ♕e8 15 ♗xb6 axb6 16 f4 with a strong White initiative, Thipsay - Inkiov, Calcutta 1986.

8   ♗g5
8 ♗e3 has been much tested recently. Now 8 ... ♗xe3?! does not look impressive for Black, e.g. 9 fxe3 0-0 (9 ... ♗g4 10 ♕d3) 10 ♗c4+ ♔h8 11 ♘g5 ♗g4 12 ♕e1! with a very pleasant position for White. Therefore, practice has seen exclusively 8 ... ♗b6 9 ♘d5 0-0 (9 ... ♘xe4!? is clearly a critical response, but nobody has given it a practical test) 10 ♗g5 ♔h8 11 a4 (11 ♗xf6 gxf6 12 ♘h4 ♘d4 {1 ... ♖g8 13 c3 ♗g4 14 ♕d2 ♕f8 15 ♗c4 ♖g5 16 ♘xb6 axb6 17 f4 ♖h5 18 g3 ♕h6 19 ♔h1 exf4 20 ♕xf4 ♘e5 21 ♗d5 ♖f8 22 ♕xh6 ♖xh6 23 ♘f5 ♖h5 24 ♘d4 c6 ½–½ Sznapik - Inkiov, Stara Zagora Zonal 1990} 13 ♗d3 c6) and now:

see following diagram

i) 11 ... ♗c5!? 12 c3 a5 13 ♗c4 ♗e6!? 14 ♘xf6 gxf6 15 ♗xe6 fxg5 16 ♗g4 ♕f6 17 ♕e2 ♘e7 18 ♘d2? (Not what

the position is calling for. This loses time and allows Black's kingside initiative to develop alarming proportions. Better plans were 18 ♘e1 intending ♘d3, 18 g3!? with the follow-up in mind of ♔g2, ♖h1, h4 or 18 h3!? with the idea of regrouping the knight with ♘h2) 18 ... ♖f7! 19 ♗h5 ♖g7 20 h3 ♖ag8 21 g3 g4! 22 hxg4 (22 ♗xg4 h5) 22 ... ♘g6 23 ♘f3 ♘f4! 24 gxf4 ♕h6! 25 ♘g5 exf4! 26 ♔g2 (Perovic's analysis refutes 26 ♘f7+ with 26 ... ♖xf7 27 ♗xf7 ♕h3! 28 ♗xg8 f3 29 ♕xf3 ♕xf3 30 ♗e6 ♕g3+ 31 ♔h1 ♕h3+ 32 ♔g1 h5!-+ and 26 ♔h1 with 26 ... ♖xg5 27 f3 ♖xh5+ 28 gxh5 ♖g5 -+) 26 ... ♖xg5 27 ♔h3 ♖xh5+! 28 gxh5 ♖g5 29 ♔h4 ♕f6 30 ♔h3 f3 0-1 Abramovic – Perovic, Vienna 1989.

ii) 11 ... ♗g4?! 12 ♗e2 ♗xf3

(Another method of trying to limit White's advantage to manageable proportions is 12 ... ♘e7 13 ♗xf6 gxf6 14 ♘xe7 ♗xf3! {14 ... ♕xe7 15 ♘h4 ♗e6 16 ♗g4} 15 ♗xf3 ♕xe7 16 ♗g4) 13 ♗xf3 ♘e7 14 ♘xf6! gxf6 15 ♗h6 ♖g8 16 a5 ♗c5 17 c3 a6 18 ♗h5! ♘g6 19 ♔h1 ♕e7 20 g3 c6 21 ♕f3 ♘f8?! 22 ♖ad1 ♘e6? (Black had to try 22 ... ♖d8. The move played allows a powerful tactical response) 23 b4! ♗a7 24 ♖xd6! ♖ad8 (Also hopeless are: 24 ... ♕xd6 25 ♕xf6+ +-, 24 ... ♘g5 25 ♕xf6+ ♕xf6 26 ♖xf6 ♘xe4 27 ♖f7 +- and 24 ... ♘f4 25 ♖d2 +- as pointed out by Khalifman in his notes in *Informator*) 25 ♖fd1! ♘g7 26 ♖xd8 ♖xd8 27 ♖xd8+ ♕xd8 28 ♗f7 +- ♕e7 29 ♗c4 f5 30 exf5 ♕f6 31 ♗xg7+ ♔xg7 32 ♔g2 ♔f8 33 ♕d3 ♕e7 34 ♕d2! ♔g7 35 ♕e2 e4 36 ♗e6 ♕f6 37 ♕g4+ ♔h6 38 ♕xe4 ♕xc3 39 ♕h4+ ♔g7 40 ♕g5+ ♔f8 41 f6 1-0 Khalifman – Inkiov, Moscow GMA 1989.

iii) 11 ... ♘e7! 12 a5 ♗c5 13 ♖a4!? is an untested suggestion of Khalifman.

8 a3 is a loss of time. After 8 ... 0-0 9 ♘a4 ♗b6 10 ♘xb6 axb6 11 c3 ♔h8 12 ♖e1

♕e8 was not inspiring for White, Yudasin - Inkiov, Minsk 1982.

8 h3 is a similar waste of time which White can ill afford. Plaza - Schuermans, Thessaloniki Ol. 1988 saw White punished drastically for this indulgence: 8 ... 0-0 9 ♗c4+ ♔h8 10 ♘g5 ♕e8 11 ♘d5 ♘xd5 12 ♕xd5 ♘d8 13 ♗e3 h6 14 ♗xc5 dxc5 15 ♘f3 ♖xf3 16 gxf3 ♗xh3 17 ♔h2 ♗xf1 18 ♖xf1 ♕h5+ 19 ♔g2 ♘c6 20 c3 ♖f8 21 ♗e2 ♕g5+ 0-1.

White also gets nowhere with **8 ♕d3** 0-0 9 ♘a4. In the game Velikov - Melegehyi, Hungary 1979 there followed 9 ... ♗b6 10 ♘xb6 axb6 11 ♗xc6 bxc6 12 ♕c4+ ♔h8 13 ♕xc6 ♗d7 with a Black initiative. No better is 9 ♗g5 ♔h8 10 ♘d5. In the game Lhagva - Baumgartner, Lucerne 1982, there followed 10 ... ♘e7 (10 ... ♘b4 is possible) 11 ♘xf6 gxf6 12 ♗h6 ♖g8 13 ♗c4 ♖g6 14 ♕d2 d5!, and after 15 b4 ♗b6 16 ♔h1 c6 17 ♗d3 ♘g8 Black stood very well.

8 ... 0-0
9 ♘d5

9 ♘a4 ♗b6 10 ♘xb6 axb6 11 ♗c4+ ♔h8 fails to pose any serious threats to Black's build up on the kingside. Riefner - Bruning, Bundesliga 1990 witnessed another fiasco for White, e.g. 12 c3 ♕e8 13 ♘d2 ♕g6 14 ♗xf6 ♖xf6 15 f3 ♘e7 16 ♖f2 ♕g5 17 ♘f1 ♘g6 18 ♕d2 ♘f4 19 ♔h1 ♗d7 20 ♘e3 ♖h6 21 ♘d5 ♕g3 22 h3 ♗xh3 23 ♔g1 ♗e6 0-1.

White must be more diligent in this variation. It is essential to find a method of disrupting the easy flow of black pieces to the kingside.

9 ... ♔h8
10 ♘h4

10 c3 ♘e7 11 ♘xf6 (11 b4 ♘exd5 12 exd5 ♗b6 13 a4 a6 14 ♗e2 ♕e8∓ Rigo - Melehegyi, Topolka 1981) 11 ... gxf6 12 ♗h6 ♖g8 13 ♗c4 ♖g4 14 ♕b3 and now with 14 ... ♘g8! Black obtained the better chances, Chelushkina - Borodulina, Zhitomir 1986

10 ... ♘d4
11 ♗d3 c6

see following diagram

In this position, White must already think about trying to obtain equality. For example **12 ♘xf6** is a mistake on account of 12 ...

gxf6 13 ♗h6 ♖g8 14 c3 ♗g4 and Black stands much better. In Grunberg – Parma, Buenos Aires 1978, White tried 12 ♗xf6 gxf6 13 ♘e3 ♘e6 14 ♘ef5 ♗g7 15 ♕d2? (essential was 15 ♕h5 to keep chances for equality) 15 ... ♘xf5 16 exf5 (on 16 ♘xf5 ♗xf5 17 exf5 there would follow 17 ... d5) 16 ... ♕e7 17 ♕h6 ♔g8 18 c4 ♕g7 and Black has an edge.

A2)

6 ... d6

Previously, this move was considered essential, but compared with the variations we have already considered Black has great difficulty in obtaining equality.

7 ♘c3

Other variations are not dangerous for Black, e.g. 7 ♗c4 ♘a5 8 ♕d3 ♘xc4 9 ♕xc4 ♕e7, 7 ♗g5 ♗e7 8 ♗xf6 ♗xf6 9 ♕d5 ♗d7 10 ♘c3 ♕c8 11 ♖ad1 ♘d8 or 7 ♖e1 ♗e7 8 ♘bd2 (8 b3 0-0) 8 ... 0-0 9 ♗c4+ ♔h8 Rizhkov - Mik. Tseitlin, Kohla-Yarve 1983. Clearly White is not going to cause Black serious problems with variations from the text.

However 7 ♕d3

deserves closer attention:

a) 7 ... ♗e7 8 ♕c4 (8 ♗c4 ♘a5 9 ♖d1!) 8 ... ♕d7 (In Schmidt - Mark Tseitlin,

Leningrad 1965, Black preferred 8 ... a6, but after 9 ♗xc6+ bxc6 10 ♘c3 d5 11 ♕a4 d4 12 ♘d5 ♗d7 13 ♘xe7 ♕xe7 14 ♕a5 c5 15 ♕xc7 White was a pawn up) 9 ♘g5! ♖f8 10 ♗xc6 bxc6 11 f4!± Fischdick – Lau, Lucerne 1982.

b) 7 ... ♗d7 8 a3 ♕e7 9 ♘c3 0-0-0 10 b4 h6 11 ♗e3 g5 12 ♖fb1 preparing a strong attack against the king.

c) The best continuation for Black from the diagram is 7 ... ♗g4! Now 8 ♗g5 ♗e7 9 ♘bd2 ♕d7 10 h3 does not help White in view of 10 ... ♗h5 11 a3 h6 12 ♗e3 g5 with initiative Wolf – Tarrasch, Monte Carlo 1903.

After 8 h3 best is 8 ... ♗xf3 (8 ... ♗h5 is also possible, e.g. 9 ♘g5 h6 10 ♘e6 ♕e7 11 ♕c4 ♔d7 12 ♘xf8+ ♖hxf8 13 ♘c3 g5=) 9 ♕xf3 ♗e7 with the following possibilities:

ci) 10 ♕d3 (10 ♘c3 leads to the main variation) 10 ... 0-0 11 ♗xc6 bxc6 12 ♕c4+ d5 13 ♕xc6 ♘xe4∓

cii) 10 ♗c4 ♕d7 11 ♗g5 0-0-0 12 ♘c3 ♖df8∓ Wojtkiewicz – Yudasin, Panevezshis 1977.

ciii) 10 ♖e1 0-0 11 c3

(Matanovic – Preissman, Buenos Aires 1978) 11 ... ♔h8!, and, as in the other lines, ... h6, ... ♔h8 and ... ♗g5 with good counterplay.

Therefore, in answer to 7 ... ♗g4 theory recommends 8 ♘c3. However, as well as 8 ... ♗e7, leading to the main variation, Black has the interesting alternative 8 ... a6!? 9 ♗a4 b5 10 ♗b3 ♘a5. The game Ignatiev – Kuindzhi, Moscow 1964 continued 11 ♗g5 c6 12 ♖ad1 h6 13 ♗h4 g5 14 ♗g3 ♘xb3 15 axb3 ♘h5 16 ♕e3 ♕c7 17 ♘e2 ♘f4 18 c4 ♗e7 and Black obtained the initiative.

Instead of 8 ♘c3, Tarrasch recommended 8 a3!? intending ♗c4. S. Tatai and S. Zinser recommend 8 ... ♕d7 9 ♗c4 ♗e6? 10 ♘g5 ♗xc4 11 ♕xc4 ♘d8 but this allows the unpleasant reply 12 f4! Correct instead is 9 ... ♗e7! after which 10 ♘g5 is pointless in view of 10 ... h6! 11 ♘f3 g5.

Let's return to the main continuation after 7 ♘c3.

7   ...   ♗e7

Here the move 7 ... ♗g4 has no point, e.g 8 h3 ♗h5 9 g4 ♗g6 10 ♘g5 ♕d7 11 ♘d5 ♘xe4 12 ♘e6±

In the case of **7 ... ♗e6 8 ♘g5 ♗g8 9 f4!** gives White excellent play.

Together with the text move worthy of interest is **7 ... a6!? 8 ♗a4 b5 9 ♗b3 ♘a5**. The game Petrenko – Mik. Tseitlin, Smolensk 1986 continued 10 ♕d3 c6 11 ♗g5 h6 12 ♗d2 g5 13 ♘d1 ♘xb3 14 axb3 ♘h5 15 c4 ♖b8 16 g3 ♕f6 17 ♘e1 ♗e7 18 ♔g2 0-0 with active play for Black.

8 ♕d3

Apart from this, the normal continuation, White has a number of alternatives at his disposal:

a) **8 ♗e3** 0-0 9 ♗c4+ ♔h8 10 ♕e2 ♗g4 with good play for Black Consultants – Levin, Kiev 1902.

b) **8 a4** 0-0 9 ♗c4+ ♔h8 10 ♘g5 ♕e8 11 ♗e6 h6 12 ♗xc8 ♕xc8= Romanishin – Lombardy, Mexico 1980.

c) **8 h3** 0-0 9 ♗c4+ (9 ♗e3 ♔h8 10 ♖e1 ♗e6 11 ♗f1 ♕e8 12 ♘d5 ♗d8 13 ♘xf6 ♗xf6 14 g3 ♕h5 15 ♘d2 ♕g6 was complex with chances for both sides, Padevsky – Szymczak, Bulgaria 1975) 9 ... ♔h8 10 ♘g5 ♕e8 11 ♘e6 (after 11 f4 exf4 12 ♗xf4 ♕g6 13 ♕e2 ♘e5 Black has satisfactory play) 11 ... ♗xe6 12 ♗xe6 ♘d4 13 ♗c4 ♕g6 14 ♗e3 ♘h5 15 ♘d5 ♗d8 16 c3 ♘f3+ 17 ♔h1 ♕xe4 18 ♘xc7 ♗xc7 19 ♗d5 ♕xe3!! and Black wins, Meski – Lelchuk, Jurmala 1980.

d) **8 ♗c4 ♗g4** (possible is 8 ... ♘a5), and now as 9 ♗e3 ♕d7 10 a3 h6 11 ♗e2 g5 12 ♘d2 ♗e6 13 ♗c4 ♘d8 (Nezhmetdinov – Holmov, Moscow 1961) and 9 h3 ♗h5 10 ♕d3 ♘b4 11 ♕e2 ♗xf3 12 gxf3 ♕d7 (Mikenas – Tolush, Moscow 1957) lead to good play for Black, best is 9 ♘d5!? when 9 ... ♘xd5 10 ♗xd5 ♖f8 keeps it level.

e) **8 ♘d5 ♘xe4!?** 9 ♘xe7 (9 ♖e1 deserves attention) 9 ... ♕xe7 10 ♕d5 ♘f6 11 ♗xc6+ ♔f8! 12 ♕b5 (or 12 ♕c4 ♗e6 13 ♕a4 bxc6 14 ♕xc6 ♗d5 15 ♕c3 h6) 12 ... a6 13 ♕a4 bxc6 14 ♕xc6 ♖b8. The game Karaklajic – Wittman, Kapfenburg 1976

continued 15 ♕a4 ♔g8 16
♖e1 h6 17 c4 ♕f7 18 ♕c2 ♗b7
19 ♘d2 ♖f8∓ Instead of 8 ...
♘xe4, possible is 8 ... 0-0 9
♘g5 ♔h8!?, and after 10
♗c4 ♘xd5 11 ♘xh7 ♖f4 12
♗xf4 ♘xf4, Black had a
winning position, Mark
Tseitlin - Arbakov, Gomel
1984.

f) **8 a3** 0-0 9 ♗c4+ (9 ♕d3
♔h8 10 ♗e3 ♗g4 11 ♘d2 ♘h5
12 f3 ♗d7 13 g3 ♗g5 14 ♗xc6
bxc6 15 ♘c4 a5 16 a4 ♗e6 17
♘d1 ♕f6∓ Shishmarev -
Yudasin, Leningrad 1973) 9
... ♔h8 10 ♘g5 ♕e8 11 ♘e6
(11 f4 exf4 12 ♗xf4 ♗d8) 11
... ♗xe6 12 ♗xe6 ♘d4=,
Jasnikowsky - Lipsky, Pol-
and 1979. An alternative to
8 ... 0-0 is 8 ... ♗g4 9 h3
♗xf3 10 ♕xf3 0-0 11 ♕d3
♔h8 12 ♗e3 as in Chibur-
danidze - Gaprindashvili,
Pitsunda 1978. This game
conitnued 12 ... ♘h5 13 ♖ad1
(13 ♘d5 ♘f4) 13 ... ♗g5 14
♘d5 (if 14 ♘e2, Black can
reply 14 ... ♗xe3 or 14 ... a6)
14 ... ♗xe3 15 fxe3! ♘f6 16
♕c4± Instead of 14 ... ♗xe3,
possible are: 14 ... ♘f4 15
♗xf4 exf4 16 ♗xc6 (16 ♕c3
f3!) 16 ... bxc6 17 ♘c3 f3!
and 14 ... a6 15 ♗c4 (15 ♗xg5
♕xg5 16 ♗xc6 bxc6 17 ♘xc7?
♘f4) 15 ... ♘f4 16 ♗xf4 exf4!

8   ...   ♗g4

Insufficient is **8 ... ♗d7?!**
9 ♗c4 ♘a5 10 ♘g5 ♘xc4 11
♕xc4 ♖f8 12 f4 exf4 13
♗xf4 h6 14 ♘f3 ♘g4 15
♗d2±

9   h3

Alternatively:

a) **9 ♘d5** 0-0 10 ♘g5 ♘d4
(10 ... ♔h8!?) 11 ♗c4 ♘xd5
12 ♗xd5+ ♔h8 13 ♘f7+ ♖xf7
14 ♗xf7 ♗e2 15 ♕d2 ♕f8 16
♖e1 ♕xf7 17 ♖xe2 ♗g5=
Ledezer - Mallée, Corres-
pondence 1974.

b) **9 ♘h4** ♕d7 10 ♘f5
♗xf5 11 exf5 d5 12 ♗g5 a6 13
♗a4 0-0-0 with good play
for Black, Krasnov - Mik.
Tseitlin, Moscow 1976.

c) **9 ♗c4** ♕d7 10 a3 h6 11
♘h4 g5 12 ♘g6 ♖h7 13 ♘d5
♗d8 14 f4 gxf4∓ Kaidanov -
Mik. Tseitlin, Beltsi 1978.

d) **9 a3** 0-0 10 ♘g5 ♕e8 11
h3 ♗d7 12 ♘d5 ♗d8 13 ♗c4
♔h8. The game Suchting -

Duz - Hotimirski, Prague 1908 continued 14 ♗d2 h6 15 ♘f3 ♘e7 16 ♘xe7 ♗xe7 17 ♖ae1 ♘h5 18 ♔h2 ♘f4 19 ♗xf4 ♖xf4 with the better position for Black. In Pinkas - Mallée, Lublin 1975, Black preferred 9 ... ♘d7 10 ♘d5 0-0 11 ♗c4 ♔h8 12 ♘xe7 ♕xe7 13 ♘g5 ♘d4 14 ♖e1 h6 15 ♕g3 ♘f6 16 h3 ♗d7 17 ♘f3 ♘h5 18 ♕g6 (18 ♘h4 ♕f6) 18 ... ♘xf3+ 19 gxf3 ♕h4 20 ♗xh6 ♖xf3 with a winning position for Black.

In answer to 9 a3, Black can also continue in similar fashion to the main line, i.e. 9 ... ♗xf3 10 ♕xf3 0-0 with the following examples:

di) 11 ♕d3 ♔h8 12 ♗e3 ♘h5 13 ♘d5 (Kostro - Franzen, Stary Smokovec 1972) and now 13 ... ♘f4! 14 ♗xf4 exf4 15 ♕c3 f3∓

dii) 11 ♗c4+ ♔h8 12 ♕d3 ♘h5 13 ♘e2 ♘f4 14 ♗xf4 exf4 15 f3 ♗f6= Zatulovskaya - Gaprindashvili, Petukov Tribunalski 1979.

diii) 11 ♕d1 (11 ♕h3!?) 11 ... ♔h8 12 ♗e3 h6 13 ♔h1 ♘h7 14 f3 ♗g5 15 ♗g1 h5 16 ♘d5 ♘e7 17 ♗e2 a5 18 ♘xe7 ♕xe7 19 a4 h4 20 ♗c4 ♘f6 21 ♖a3 ♘h5∓ Malinichev - Mik. Tseitlin, Sochi 1981.

e) 9 ♕c4 ♗xf3! and the correspondence game Prajnfalk - Konstantinopolsky (1975/78) continued 10 gxf3 ♕d7 11 ♘d5 a6 12 ♗xc6 bxc6 13 ♘xe7 (or 13 ♘b4 c5 14 ♘d5 ♘xd5 15 ♕xd5 c6, and Black begins the counterattack) 13 ... ♔xe7 14 ♗g5 ♖hf8 15 ♔h1 ♕h3 16 ♕e2 (16 ♕c3 ♔d7 17 ♖fd1 ♕h5) 16 ... h6, with active Black play.

Preferable to 10 gxf3 is 10 ♗xc6+ bxc6 11 ♕xc6+ ♕d7! 12 ♕xd7+ (certainly not 12 ♕xa8+? ♔f7 and White loses the queen) 12 ... ♔xd7 13 gxf3. Here, however, after 13 ... ♘h5, Black has sufficient compensation for the pawn, e.g. 14 ♖d1 (14 ♘e2 ♖hf8) 14 ... ♖hf8 15 ♖d3 ♖f6! Instead of 15 ... ♖f6!, 15 ... ♖f7 is inaccurate as can be seen from the correspondence game Mik. Tseitlin - Banfalvi (1985/89) which continued 16 ♘e2 ♖af8 17 ♔g2 ♖f6 18 ♘g3 g6 19 ♖b3 ♘f4+ 20 ♗xf4 ♖xf4 21 ♖d1 h5 22 ♖dd3 ♖a8 23 c4 a5 24 c5 and White obtained the initiative.

Returning to the position after 9 h3:

9 ... ♗xf3
10 ♕xf3 0-0

11 ♕d1

On 11 ♕d3 ♔h8 12 ♗e3 can follow 12 ... ♘h5 13 ♘d5 ♘f4 14 ♗xf4 exf4 15 ♕c3 f3 or 12 ... ♘b4 13 ♕d2 c6 14 ♗e2 d5 in both cases with good Black play.

11 ...   ♔h8
12 ♗e3   h6!

This continuation has been worked out by Mik. Tseitlin. The game Pilnik - Rubinetti, Mar del Plata 1971 saw a weaker response from Black, 12 ... ♕e8?! and after 13 ♘d5! ♗d8 14 ♘xf6 ♗xf6 (14 ... ♖xf6!?) 15 c3 ♕g6 16 ♕g4 ♕xg4 17 hxg4 h6 18 g3 White had all the chances.

Here, Black is threatening to take the initiative on

the kingside. Grigorov - Mik. Tseitlin, Pernik 1977 continued 13 ♕d2 ♘h7 14 ♘d5 ♗g5 15 f4 exf4 16 ♘xf4 ♗xf4 17 ♗xf4 ♘e5 18 ♗xe5

dxe5 19 ♕xd8 ♖axd8 20 ♖xf8+ ♖xf8 21 ♖f1 ♖xf1+ 22 ♔xf1 ♘f6. In this resultant position, the Black knight is stronger than the opposing bishop.

Also good for Black was Solovyev - Mik. Tseitlin, Cheliabinsk 1980 which continued 13 a3 ♘h7 14 ♘e2 ♗g5 15 f4 exf4 16 ♘xf4 ♗xf4 17 ♗xf4 ♕h4 18 ♕d2 ♘e5 19 ♖ae1 ♘g5 20 ♗xg5 hxg5! 21 ♖xf8+ ♖xf8 22 ♖f1 ♖f4! 23 ♕d5 ♕g3 with a winning position for Black.

B

4   ...   ♘f6

Here, we have to consider two main variations:

B1) 5 0-0
B2) 5 exf5

5 ♘c3 does not present Black with any problems,

e.g. 5 ... ♗b4! 6 0-0 ♗xc3 7 bxc3 fxe4 8 dxe4 d6 (8 ... 0-0 9 ♕e2 ♕e8 10 ♘e1 d6 11 f3 ♗d7 12 ♗c4+ ♔h8 13 ♗e3 ♘a5 also gives Black no cause for complaint) and now:

a) 9 ♖e1 0-0 10 ♖b1 ♔h8 11 ♗g5 ♕e8 12 ♕d2 ♗d7 Slivin - Nadezhdin, Rostov 1960.

b) 9 ♘d2 0-0 10 ♗d3 ♕e8 11 ♘c4 ♗d8 12 ♘e3 ♘e6 13 ♘d5 ♘xd5 14 exd5 ♘f4 15 c4 b6 16 f3 ♕h5 17 ♗e3 ♗d7 18 ♕d2 ♖f6∓ Polovodin - Arbakov, "Zenit" Ch. 1981.

c) 9 ♕d3 (note also 9 ♗g5 ♗e6 10 ♘h4 h6!) 9 ... ♗d7 (also good are 9 ... ♕e7 10 ♘h4 0-0 and 9 ... 0-0 10 ♕c4+ ♔h8 11 ♗xc6 bxc6 12 ♕xc6 ♗g4 13 ♘d2 ♘h5 14 f3 ♗d7 15 ♕c4 ♘f4 16 ♖f2 ♖b8 17 ♕f1 ♕g5 with a strong intitiative for the pawn, Zolotonos - Korelov, Leningrad 1973. 10 ♗g5 (10 ♖b1 ♘a5 11 ♗xd7+ ♕xd7 12 ♗g5 ♕c6 13 ♗xf6 gxf6 14 ♘h4 0-0-0 15 ♘f5 ♖d7 16 ♘e3 ♖g8∓ Teichmann - Marshall, Monte Carlo 1902) 10 ... h6 11 ♗xf6 ♕xf6 12 c4 a6 13 ♗a4 0-0-0 14 ♖ab1 ♘b8 15 ♗xd7+ ♘xd7 16 ♘d2 ♘c5 and Black is better, Nash - Liublinsky, Correspondence 1963.

B1

5 0-0 ♗c5
6 ♘c3

6 ♘xe5 ♘xe5 7 d4 ♘xe4!? with sharp play.

6 ♗xc6 dxc6 7 ♘xe5 fxe4 8 dxe4 ♕xd1 9 ♖xd1 ♘xe4 10 ♗e3 ♗xe3 11 fxe3 0-0∓ (Fleissig).

6 ♗c4 leads to a position from the King's Gambit Declined with colours reversed. As well as 6 ... fxe4 7 dxe4 d6, which leads to a position examined in part A (note to White's sixth move), Black can play 6 ... d6 immediately.

And now:

a) **7 ♘g5** f4 8 ♘f7 ♕e7 9 ♘xh8 ♗g4 10 ♕d2 ♘d4 11 ♔h1 ♘f3! 12 ♕a5 ♘xe4! - a beautiful conclusion to Black's attack, Balla - Reti, Budapest 1918.

b) **7 ♗e3** ♗xe3 8 fxe3 ♘a5 9 ♗b3 ♘xb3 10 axb3 fxe4 11

dxe4 ♘xe4 12 ♘xe5 ♘f6!∓

c) **7 ♗g5** h6 8 ♗xf6 ♕xf6 9 c3 f4 10 ♘bd2 g5 11 ♘b3 ♗b6 12 a4 a5 13 ♗b5 ♗d7 14 d4 g4 with a strong attack, Minckwitz - Anderssen, Berlin 1866.

d) **7 h3** ♘a5 8 ♗g5 ♘xc4 9 dxc4 h6 10 ♗xf6 ♕xf6 11 ♘c3 a6 12 ♘d5 ♕f7 13 exf5 ♗xf5 14 ♘h4 ♗h7 15 ♔h1 0-0∓ Breyer - Hromadka, Baden 1914.

e) **7 ♘c3** f4! 8 h3 ♘d4! and Black's chances are preferable, e.g. 9 ♘a4 9 ... ♘xf3+ 10 ♕xf3 g5, 9 ♘d5 ♘xd5 10 ♗xd5 ♘xf3+ 11 ♕xf3 ♕h4, or finally, 9 ♘xd4 ♗xd4 10 ♘d5 (10 ♘a4? a6) 10 ... ♘xd5 11 ♗xd5 ♕h4 12 c3 ♗b6 13 d4 ♖f8.

6   ...   0-0

The natural move 6 ... **d6** encountered an unexpected refutation in the game Berger - Duz Hotimirski, Carlsbad 1907, i.e. 7 exf5! 0-0 (or 7 ... ♗xf5 8 d4) 8 ♘e4 ♗b6 9 ♘g3 ♘e7 10 ♗c4+ d5 11 ♗b3 ♕d6 12 ♕e2 ♘d7 13 ♘e4! ♕c6 14 ♘c3 with a winning position for White.

7   ♗g5

7 ♗c4+ ♔h8 8 ♘g5 d6 (8 ... ♕e7!?) 9 ♘f7+ ♖xf7 10 ♗xf7 f4 11 ♗h5 g5 12 ♘d5

♗e6= Tarasov - Tsarev, Moscow 1973.

7   ...   d6

Possible is 7 ... **h6** to meet 8 ♗xf6 ♕xf6 9 ♘d5 ♕d8 10 c3 with 10 ... fxe4 11 dxe4 a6, or immediately 10 ... a6 with approximately equal chances.

J. Belavenets recommends the immediate 7 ... **a6**.

8   ♗c4+

The exchange 8 **♗xc6** is illogical. The correspondence game Schiffers - Hardin, (1897/98) continued bxc6 9 d4 exd4 10 ♘xd4 ♕d7 (also worth attention is 10 ... ♕e8! 11 ♖e1 ♕g6) 11 ♗xf6 ♖xf6 12 exf5 and after 12 ... d5! 13 ♖e1 ♕f7 14 ♕d2 ♗xf5 15 ♘xf5 ♖xf5 16 ♖e2 ♖f8 17 ♖f1 ♕h5 Black had the advantage.

A consultation game from 1899 saw 8 ♘e2 but after 8 ... ♕e8 9 exf5 ♗xf5 10 d4 exd4 11 ♘exd4 ♗g4 12 ♕d3 ♕h5! 13 ♘xc6 ♗xf3 the complications favoured Black.

8 ♘d5 is met favourably by 8 ... fxe4.

8   ...   ♔h8
9   ♘d5   ♘a5!

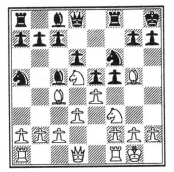

Black's chances are to be preferred here. On 10 ♘xf6 10 ... gxf6 11 ♗h6 there follows 11 ... ♘xc4! 12 ♗xf8 fxe4 13 dxc4 exf3 14 ♗h6 ♗g4∓, and in the event of **10 exf5** ♘xc4 11 dxc4 ♗xf5 is also better for Black (Schiffers - Hardin, Correspondence 1894).

B2)

	4	...	♘f6
	5	exf5	♗c5

The little known game Pavlov - Alekhine, Moscow 1920 is worthy of attention: 5 ... ♗e7 6 ♗xc6 dxc6 7 ♘xe5 ♗xf5 8 0-0 0-0 9 f4 ♕d4+ 10 ♔h1 ♖ad8 11 ♘d2 ♕d5 12 ♘df3 ♗c5 13 ♕e1 ♖de8 14 ♕g3 ♖e6 15 ♗d2 ♘h5 16 ♕e1 ♗g4 with sufficient compensation for the pawn.

The original 5 ... ♘e7!? led to equal chances after 6

0-0 c6 7 ♗c4 d6 8 ♖e1 ♗xf5 9 ♗g5 ♕d7 10 ♘c3 h6 11 ♗xf6 gxf6 12 d4 e4 13 ♘h4 d5 14 ♘e2 ♗e6 in Kindermann - Geenen, Thessaloniki 1988.

    6   ♘c3

Black has no problems after **6 ♘xe5** 0-0 (possible is 6 ... ♘d4) 7 ♘xc6 because of 7 ... ♖e8+ 8 ♔f1 dxc6 9 ♗c4+ ♔h8.

After **6 0-0**, Black should answer 6 ... 0-0 leading to the following position:

Here White has the following possibilities at his disposal:

a) **7 ♗xc6** dxc6 8 ♘xe5 (a

very risky plan) 8 ... ♗xf5. The game Burba - Havuchek, Prague 1961 continued 9 ♘c3 ♕e8 (9 ... ♗d4 10 ♘c4 ♘g4 11 ♘e3 ♕h4 is recommended by ECO) 10 ♖e1 ♘g4 11 ♘xg4 ♗xg4 12 ♖xe8 ♖axe8! and Black wins as a queen move is met by 13 ... ♖xf2.

In the game Göring – Minckwitz, Leipzig 1871 White chose 9 ♗e3 ♕e7 10 d4 ♖ad8 11 c3 ♗d6 12 ♘c4 (better is 12 f4), and there followed a standard sacrifice, 12 ... ♗xh2+! 13 ♔xh2 ♘g4+ 14 ♔g1 (if 14 ♔g3 b5 and ... ♕d6+) 14 ... ♕h4 15 ♗f4 ♗e4 16 ♗g3 ♖xf2 17 ♗xh4 ♖xg2+ 18 ♔h1 ♖h2+ 19 ♔g1 ♖h1+ mate. A graceful miniature.

b) 7 ♘xe5 (7 ♘c3 leads to the main variation) 7 ... ♘xe5 8 d4 ♗xd4 9 ♕xd4 d6 and the game Shiyanovsky – Gipslis, Riga 1955 soon ended as a draw.

c) 7 ♗e3 (strongest according to ECO) 7 ... ♘d4! 8 c3 ♘xf3+ 9 ♕xf3 ♗e7. The correspondence game Itkin – Glazkov (1985) continued thus: 10 ♘d2 c6 11 ♗a4 d5 12 ♗b3 ♘e8 13 g4 g6 14 ♗h6 and now with the move 14 ... ♘g7! Black could obtain a good position. On 10 g4 c6 11 ♗a4 d5 12 ♘d2 could follow 12 ... h5 13 h3 hxg4 14 hxg4 ♘xg4 15 ♕xg4 ♗xf5 16 ♕e2 ♖f6 with a strong Black attack, typical of this variation.

6 ... 0-0

7 0-0

7 ♘e4 ♗e7 8 0-0 d5 9 ♘g3 ♗d6 10 ♖e1 ♘d4 11 ♗a4 ♘xf3+ 12 ♕xf3 e4 with a strong initiative, Chiburdanidze – Kantorovich, Moscow 1965.

In the event of 7 ♗g5 ♘d4 8 ♗a4 c6 9 0-0 d5 10 ♘xe5 ♗xf5 Black also has good play. Instead of 8 ♗a4, the correspondence game Kryukov – Estrin (1961) saw 8 ♗c4+ ♔h8 9 0-0 c6 10 ♘e4 ♘xf3+ 11 ♕xf3 ♗e7 12 ♗xf6 ♗xf6 13 ♘d6 ♕e7 14 ♘xc8 ♖axc8 15 ♗b3 ♗g5 with good chances.

7 ... ♘d4

see following diagram

7 ... d5 is an interesting alternative. Padevsky – Popov, Bulgaria 1959 continued 8 ♗g5 ♔h8! 9 ♗xc6 bxc6 10 ♘xe5 ♗xf5 11 d4

♗d6 (better is 11 ... ♕e8, as White could now play 12 ♘xc6 ♕e8 13 ♘e5) 12 ♘e2 ♕e8 13 ♗xf6 gxf6, and after 14 ♘d3 ♖b8 15 ♕d2 ♕g6 16 ♘g3 ♖g8 17 b3 h5 Black had a good attacking position.

8 ♘xe5

After **8 ♘e4** Black can answer 8 ... ♗e7.

8 ... d5!

A natural continuation at first sight is **8 ... c6 9 ♗a4 d5** but this allows the unpleasant reply 10 ♘e2! Karpov - Bellon, Montilla 1976 went 10 ... ♕a5 (somewhat better is 10 ... ♕c7) 11 ♗b3 ♕c7 12 ♘xd4 ♕xe5 13 ♘e2! ♕xf5 14 ♘g3 ♕g6 15 d4 ♗d6 16 c3 ♘g4 17 f4 ♕h6 18 h3 and Black had no compensation for the pawn.

9 ♘f3

After **9 ♗a4 ♗xf5** Black has good chances for an attack on the king's wing. For example:

a) **10 ♘e2 ♗g4** with dangerous play.

b) **10 ♗f4** c6 11 ♘e2 ♗g4! 12 ♘xg4 ♘xg4 13 ♗g3 (13 ♘xd4? ♖xf4 14 ♘e6 ♕h4) 13 ... ♘f5 14 d4 ♘xg3 15 fxg3 (15 ♘xg3 ♕h4 16 h3 ♘xf2) 15 ... ♕g5 with a strong attack Tringov - Grunfeld, Skara 1980.

c) **10 ♗g5** c6 11 h3 (after 11 ♘e2 ♕e7 12 ♘xd4 there will follow 12 ... ♗xd4 13 ♘f3 ♗xb2) 11 ... ♕c7. In the game Kagan - Wedberg, Lucerne 1979 White answered 12 ♘f3? but after 12 ... ♗g4! soon had to capitulate. Instead of 12 ♘f3? better is 12 ♖e1 ♖ae8 13 ♗f4! ♗d6 14 ♘e2 ♘e6 15 d4 ♘xf4 16 ♘xf4 ♗xe5 17 dxe5 ♖xe5, but even here, Black's position is fine.

9	...	c6
10	♘xd4	♗xd4

Practical examples from

this position are:

a) **11 ♗a4 ♗xf5 12 ♗g5 a5 13 a3 b5 14 ♗b3 ♖a7 15 ♕d2 ♕b6 16 ♖ae1 b4 17 axb4 axb4 18 ♘d1 ♘g4** and Black's active piece play fully compensates for the missing pawn, Sudoplatov – Berezin, Moscow 1957.

b) **11 ♘e2 ♗b6 12 ♗a4 ♗xf5 13 ♗f4 ♘h5 14 ♗g3 ♗g4 15 ♕d2 ♘xg3 16 ♘xg3 ♕h4** with a strong attack, Zhmarev – Kosterin, Kiev 1958.

4)   4 d4

1	e4	e5
2	♘f3	♘c6
3	♗b5	f5
4	d4	

Whte players choosing this double-edged continuation must be prepared to sacrifice a piece.

    4 ... fxe4

4 ... ♘xd4 5 ♘xd4 exd4 6 ♕xd4 fxe4 is a weak alternative. Kupfer - Gulbrandsen, Denmark v Norway continued 7 0-0! ♘f6 8 ♗g5 c6 9 ♗xf6 ♕xf6 10 ♕xe4+ ♗e7 and now with the move 11 ♘c3! White could get the advantage.

After **4 ... exd4** 5 e5! there arises a position from the Falkbeer Countergambit with colours reversed and an extra tempo for White.

White now has two alternatives:

A) 5 ♗xc6
B) 5 ♘xe5

A)

    5 ♗xc6 dxc6

The usual reaction to White's capture, but possible is **5 ... bxc6**. The game Schiffers - Hardin, Samara 1895 saw 6 ♘xe5 ♘f6 7 0-0 ♗e7 (Tchigorin recommended 7 ... ♗b7 8 ♘c3 d5 9 f3 exf3 10 ♕xf3 ♗e7=) 8 ♘c3 ♗b7 9 ♗g5 0-0 10 ♕e2 and now the move 10 ... d6 equalises the play.

Instead of 7 0-0, 7 ♗g5 ♗e7 8 ♘d2 0-0 9 ♕e2 ♕e8 10 0-0, allowed Black good counterplay after 10 ... a5 11 ♖fe1 ♗a6 12 c4 d6 13 ♘d3 d5 14 b3 ♗d6 15 ♘c5 ♗c8 16 ♘f1 ♕g6 17 ♗xf6 ♕xf6 18 ♖ad1 ♕h4 19 g3 ♕f6 in Savasky – Banfalvi, Budapest 1981.

6   ♘xe5

6   ...   ♕h4

The most usual move, but also worthy of attention is **6 ... ♘f6**. White's most common response is 7 ♗g5 with the following possibilities:

a) **7 ... ♗e7** 8 ♘c3 0-0 9 0-0 ♗f5 10 ♕d2 h6= Kupper – Boey, Lugano 1968.

b) **7 ... c5** 8 ♘c3 ♗f5 9 f4 (Shenmann – Lublinsky, Correspondence 1960) and now with 9 ... ♕xd4 10 ♕xd4 cxd4 11 ♘b5 ♗b4+ 12 ♔f1 0-0 Black could get good counterplay.

c) **7 ... ♗f5** 8 0-0 ♗d6 9 ♘c3 h6 10 ♗h4 g5! 11 ♗g3 h5! 12 h4 ♘g4 (12 ... ♗g4!?) 13 ♕e2 gxh4 14 ♗f4 ♕f6 15 ♘xe4 ♗xe4 16 ♕xe4 0-0-0 with a dangerous Black attack, Zeitler – Milousov, Pula 1972.

d) **7 ... ♗d6** 8 ♘d2 0-0 9 0-0 (if 9 ♕e2 ♕e8 10 0-0-0 then 10 ... c5!) 9 ... ♕e8 10 f4 ♘d5! 11 ♕e2. Alipov – Chekhlov, Vilnius 1982 now saw 11 ... h6 12 ♗h4 ♖xf4 13 ♖xf4 ♘xf4 14 ♕xe4 ♗xe5 15 dxe5 (15 ♕xe5 ♕xe5 16 dxe5 ♗f5 17 ♖f1 g5 or 17 c3 ♘d3, in both cases with a Black advantage) 15 ... ♘g6 16 ♗g3 ♗e6 17 c4 ♖d8 18 ♘f1 ♗f7 19 ♖e1 ♕e6 20 b3 ♘e7 21 ♘e3 ♗g6 22 ♕h4 ♖d2 23 ♘g4 ♘f5∓.

Considering the above material, a preferable reply to 6 ... ♘f6 would appear to be 7 0-0 ♗d6 8 ♘c3 (after 8 ♕e2, Jaenisch recommended 8 ... 0-0 9 ♕c4+ ♘d5 10 ♘c3 ♗e6 with an excellent Black position). If now 8 ... 0-0 then 9 ♖e1! (worse is 9 ♕e2 ♕e8! 10 ♗f4 ♘d5!) 9 ... ♗b4 10 ♗g5 ♕e8 11 ♗xf6 gxf6 12 ♘d3! ♗xc3 13 bxc3 ♕g6 14 ♘f4 ♕f5 15 ♕d2 b5

16 f3 exf3 17 gxf3 ♘d7 18 ♔h1= Hecht - Hennings, Helsinki 1972. Hasidovsky - Nadezhdin, Tashkent 1960, saw instead 8 ... ♕e7 9 ♗g5 ♗f5 and after 10 ♗xf6 ♕xf6 11 ♕h5+ g6 12 ♕e2 ♗xe5 13 dxe5 ♕xe5 14 g4 ♗e6 15 ♕xe4 ♕xe4 16 ♘xe4 0-0-0 17 f3 ♗d5 the chances were equal. An inferior alternative to 9 ♗g5 is 9 f4?! 0-0 10 ♖e1. Pavlov - Ivanov, 1976 continued 10 ... ♗f5 11 g4 (11 h3 is more circumspect) 11 ... ♗xe5! 12 fxe5 (12 gxf5 ♗d6) 12 ... ♘xg4 13 ♘xe4 ♕h4 14 ♗f4 ♗xe4 15 ♗g3 ♕h3 16 ♖xe4 ♖f2! and White resigned.

7 ♕e2

7 ♗e3 ♗d6 8 ♘c3 (weaker is 8 ♕d2 ♗e6 9 ♗g5 ♕h5 10 ♘c3 ♘f6 11 ♗e2 0-0-0 with the better play for Black, Zuckerman - Lazard, Paris 1929) 8 ... ♗e6 9 ♕e2! ♘f6 10 h3 0-0 11 g3 ♕h5 12 ♕xh5 ♘xh5 13 ♘g4 ♖ae8 14 0-0-0 ♗d5 15 b3 b5 ½ : ½ Estrin - Boey, 1979.

After 7 0-0, Furman and Taimanov recommend 7 ... ♗d6 8 f3 exf3 9 ♘xf3 ♕h5. Georgadze - Mik. Tseitlin, Simferopol 1975 continued 10 ♘c3 ♘e7 11 ♘e4 0-0 12 ♘xd6 cxd6 13 ♕e1 ♘g6

which was fine for Black.

Instead of 7 ... ♗d6, 7 ... ♘f6 leads to the following position:

Here the following possibilities must be considered:

a) **8 f4** ♗f5 9 c4 0-0-0 10 ♗e3 ♘g4 11 ♘xg4 ♗xg4 12 ♕e1 ♕h5 13 ♘c3 ♗b4∓ Vukevic - Baretic, Belgrade 1963.

b) **8 ♗e3** ♗d6 9 ♕d2 ♗e6 10 ♘c3 0-0-0 and Black has comfortable play (Bilguer).

c) **8 ♘c3** ♗d6 9 ♕e2 ♗e6 10 f4 ♗f5 11 ♗e3 0-0 12 ♖ae1 ♖ae8∓ Durao - Alexander, Dublin 1957.

d) **8 f3** ♗d6 9 ♕e1 ♕h5 10 ♘c3 ♗xe5 11 dxe5 ♕xe5 12 ♘xe4= Rellstab - Tolush, Vienna 1957.

7 ... ♘f6!

P. Keres recommended 7 ... ♗e6 8 h3 0-0-0 9 g3 ♕e7, as the capture 10 ♕xe4 is very risky on account of 10 ... ♘f6 11 ♕f4 ♕d6 and with 12 ... c5 and 12 ... g5 in the air, White has great difficulties. However, White shouldn't accept this poisoned pawn. The correspondence game Grabowsky - Wittman, 1976/77 shows the correct path: 10 ♗e3! (preventing ... c5) 10 ... ♘f6 11 ♘c3 ♕b4 12 0-0-0 c5 13 a3 ♕a5 14 d5! ♘xd5 (if 14 ... ♗d7 then 15 ♘f7 and after 14 ... ♗g8 15 ♘xe4 follows) 15 ♘xd5 ♖xd5 16 ♖xd5 ♗xd5 17 ♕g4+ with a winning position for White, as 17 ... ♔b8 is answered by 18 ♘d7+ ♔a8 19 ♕h5!

Taking this into account, 8 ... ♗d6! (instead of 8 ... 0-0-0) deserves consideration. Cardoso - Boey, Skopje 1972 continued 9 ♘c3 ♘f6 10 g3 ♕h5 11 g4 (better is 11 ♕xh5+ ♘xh5 12 ♘g4 with equality) 11 ... ♕h4 12 ♗f4 and after 12 ... ♗xg4! 13 ♘xg4 ♗xf4 14 ♘xf6+ ♕xf6 15 ♘xe4 ♕e7 16 ♘c5 ♕xe2+ 17 ♔xe2 0-0-0 Black had all the chances.

8 h3

8 ♘c3 ♗b4 (8 ... ♗e6 intending ... ♗d6 is probably an improvement) 9 0-0 ♗xc3 10 bxc3 0-0 11 ♖b1 a5

12 c4 ♘g4 13 ♘xg4 ♗xg4 14 ♕e3 ♗e6 15 ♖xb7 ♗xc4 16 ♖e1 ♗xa2 17 ♖xc7 ♗d5 18 ♗a3 ♖f7= Vasiliev - Mik. Tseitlin, Dubna 1981.

8 ♘d2 ♗f5 9 ♘f1 ♗e6 10 ♘g3 0-0-0 11 ♗e3 ♗d6 12 ♗d2 ♖he8 13 0-0-0 ♗xe5∓ Sudnitsin - Glazkov, Moscow 1973.

Here Black doesn't stand worse and has many interesting possibilities. For example:

a) 8 ... ♘d5 9 g3 ♕f6 10 c4 ♘b6 11 a3 (11 ♘c3 ♗b4 12 ♗d2 ♗xc3 13 ♗xc3 is well met by 13 ... 0-0! and if 14 d5, then 14 ... ♕f5 with good play) 11 ... c5 12 ♗e3 ♗d6 13 ♘d2 (Markov - Hardin, Peterburg 1895) and now 13 ... ♗f5! would be strong as on 14 g4? there follows 14 ... cxd4! with the advantage.

b) 8 ... ♗d6 9 ♕c4 (better

9 ♘c3 ♗e6, leading to a position from Cardoso – Boey, which is examined in the notes to Black's seventh move) 9 ... ♕h5! and the threat of 10 ... ♗e5 means that White has difficulties, e.g. 10 ♘xc6 ♗d7 11 ♘b4 a5, 10 g4 ♘xg4! or, finally, 10 ♗f4 ♘d5 11 g4 ♗xg4! – in all cases with a Black advantage.

c) **8 ... ♗e6** 9 g3 ♕h5 10 ♕xh5+ (10 g4 ♕h4 11 ♗f4 ♘d5 12 ♕xe4 ♘xf4 13 ♕xf4 0-0-0 with good compensation for the pawn) 10 ... ♘xh5 11 0-0 ♗xh3 12 ♖e1 ♘f6 13 ♗g5 ♗e7∓ Butichin – Glazkov, Moscow 1986.

d) **8 ... ♗e7** 9 ♘c3 0-0 10 ♕c4+ (10 g3 ♕h5 11 g4 ♕h4 12 ♗f4 ♘d5!) 10 ... ♘d5 11 g3 ♕f6 12 ♘xe4 ♕f5 13 ♕e2 c5 14 ♘xc5?! (better is 14 ♗d2 cxd4 15 ♘d3) 14 ... ♗xc5 15 dxc5 ♘b4 16 ♘d3 (16 0-0 ♘xc2 17 ♖b1 ♘d4) 16 ... ♘xc2+ and Black won quickly, Geissert – Mohring, GDR 1963.

B)

5   ♘xe5   ♘xe5

The main continuation leading to very double-edged positions. However, a quieter alternative is available, e.g. **5 ... ♘f6** 6 0-0 ♗e7 7 c3 (7 ♗g5 0-0 8 ♘c3 leads nowhere in view of 8 ... ♕e8! 9 ♖e1 ♗b4!) 7 ... ♘b8! 8 ♕b3 (8 ♗g5 c6 9 ♗xf6 ♗xf6 10 ♕h5+ g6 11 ♘xg6 hxg6 12 ♕xg6+ ♔f8) 8 ... ♖f8 9 ♗g5 c6 10 ♗e2 d6 11 ♘c4 d5 and White has nothing special.

6   dxe5   c6

7   ♘c3

This piece sacrifice is more or less forced as the alternatives are rather unpalatable for White. The following are practical examples:

a) **7 ♗c4 ♕a5+** and now:

ai) **8 ♘c3 ♕xe5** 9 ♗xg8 ♖xg8 10 ♗e3 d5 11 ♕d2 ♗e6 12 0-0-0 ♗b4 van den Bosch – Spielmann, Noordwijk 1938.

aii) **8 ♘d2 ♕xe5** 9 ♗xg8 ♖xg8 10 ♕e2 d5 11 f3 ♗e6 12 fxe4 0-0-0 13 0-0 ♗c5+ 14

♔h1 ♜gf8 15 ♘f3 ♕xe4! Holmov - Bronstein, Moscow 1949.

aiii) **8 ♝d2 ♕xe5 9 ♝xg8 ♜xg8 10 ♘c3 d5 11 ♕e2 ♝d6 12 0-0-0 ♝d7 13 f3 0-0-0 14 fxe4 ♜de8** Kornusevich - Karpov Moscow 1967.

b) **7 ♝e2 ♕a5+ 8 ♘d2** (8 ♝d2 ♕xe5 9 ♝h5+ ♔d8 10 0-0 ♘f6 11 ♝e3 ♕e6!) **8 ... ♕xe5 9 ♘c4 ♕e6 10 ♝g5 ♘f6∓** Ubilava - Mik. Tseitlin, Cheliabinsk 1975.

c) **7 0-0** (a less promising sacrifice than that of the text) **7 ... cxb5 8 ♘c3 d5 9 exd6 ♕xd6 10 ♕h5+** (in response to 10 ♘xb5 Tchigorin recommended 10 ... ♕c5!) **10 ... g6 11 ♕xb5+ ♝d7 12 ♕xb7 ♕c6** and White has minimal compensation for the piece, Marco - Marshall, Monte Carlo 1902.

7   ...   cxb5
If 7 ... ♕a5 good is 8 0-0!

♝b4 9 ♘xe4. Kinnmark - Baretic, Hastings 1963/64 saw further 9 ... ♕xb5 10 c3 ♝e7 11 ♜e1 ♕d5 12 ♕h5+ ♔d8 13 ♝f4 h6 14 ♕g6 ♝f8 15 ♘d6! with a winning position for White.

After **7 ... d5 8 exd6 ♘f6 9 ♝g5 cxb5** leads to a favourable variation of the text (from Black's point of view). Thus White does better to resist the temptation to sacrifice a piece and play more quietly with 9 ♝c4 and after **9 ... ♝xd6 10 ♝g5 ♝f5** we arrive at the following position:

Now:

a) **11 ♕d4 h6! 12 ♝e3 ♕e7 13 0-0-0 ♝e5 14 ♕c5 ♕xc5 15 ♝xc5 ♘d7 16 ♝d4 0-0-0=** Belousov - Krikunov, 1977.

b) **11 ♕e2 ♕e7 12 0-0-0 0-0-0 13 h3 ♜he8 14 ♕e3 ♝c5 15 ♜xd8+ ♜xd8 16 ♕f4 ♝g6=** Belousov - Hermlin,

1977. An alternative to 13 h3 is 13 f3!? Koifman - Krikunov, 1977 continued 13 ... ♖he8!, as the follow-up 14 fxe4 ♗g6! 15 ♖he1 ♕e5! yields sufficient compensation for a pawn, and in the event of 14 ♖he1 h6 15 ♗xf6 ♕xf6 16 ♘xe4 ♗xe4 17 fxe4 ♕g5+ 18 ♔b1 ♗xh2 the chances are equal.

Of interest is the recent development 7 ... ♕e7!? 8 0-0 cxb5. If White now tries 9 ♘xe4, then 9 ... ♕e6 10 ♖e1 ♔d8! 11 ♕f3 (11 ♘d6 ♔c7) 11 ... ♘h6 and Black can hold the extra piece without too much trouble. Golubtsov - Anuhin, 1986 saw instead 9 ♗f4 ♕c5 10 ♘xe4 ♕c6 11 ♖e1 b6, and after 12 ♕f3 ♗e7 13 ♘d6+ ♗xd6 14 exd6+ ♔f8 15 ♖e4 ♘f6 16 ♖ae1 ♗b7 17 ♗h6 ♕xd6 Black had repulsed the attack, maintaining his extra piece. Preferable to 12 ♕f3 is 12 ♕h5+! ♔d8 13 ♖ad1! (not 13 ♕f7 ♘h6 14 ♗xh6 gxh6 15 ♖ad1 ♗e7 16 e6 ♖f8 17 ♕xh7 ♕xe6 when there is no effective continuation of the attack) 13 ... g6 14 ♕h3 h6!? 15 e6 ♖h7 16 ♕g4! and Black's situation is critical.

This whole variation deserves serious research. Returning to the main continuation after the Black capture 7 ... cxb5:

8 ♘xe4 d5
9 exd6 ♘f6

Worthy of attention is 9 ... ♗f5 10 ♕d5 (10 ♕e2 ♔f7) 10 ... ♕d7 11 0-0. In Gudens - Schneider, Berlin 1902, Black's response was standard: 11 ... ♘f6?, and after 12 ♘xf6+ gxf6 13 ♖e1+ ♔d8 14 ♗f4 White had obtained an overwhelming position for the sacrificed piece. Instead 11 ... ♗xe4 12 ♕xe4+ ♔f7 13 ♕d5+ ♔g6 14 ♕e4+ ♔f7 leads to a draw by repetition.

However, Black has one further interesting possibility, i.e. 11 ... ♘e7!? 12 ♕e5 ♗xe4. If now 13 ♖e1 then 13 .... 0-0-0; if 13 dxe7 ♕xe7 14 ♕xe7+ ♗xe7 15 ♖e1 0-0-0 16 h3 ♖hf8!-+ and finally 13 ♕xe4 ♕xd6 14 ♗f4 (14 ♕xb7 ♕c6) 14 ... ♕c6 15 ♕e5 ♖d8 and Black has sufficient defensive resources.

see following diagram

Here the following three alternatives deserve consideration:

B1) 10 0-0
B2) 10 ♕d4
B3) 10 ♘g5

If instead **10 ♕e2**, 10 ...
♔f7 is a good reply, e.g. 11
♗g5 ♕a5+ 12 ♗d2 b4 13 0-0
♘xe4 14 ♕xe4 ♗xd6 15 a3
♕f5 16 ♕h4 bxa3 0 : 1 Ross-
mann - Mohring, GDR 1982.

B1
10   0-0   ♘xe4
According to Keres, **10 ...
♔f7 11 ♗g5 ♗f5** deserves
attention. However, doubtful is **10 ... ♗f5?!** in view of
11 ♘xf6+ ♕xf6 12 ♖e1+ ♔f7
(after 12 ... ♔d8 13 ♗f4 ♖c8
14 ♕d5 h6 15 ♖ad1 ♗d7 16
♗e5 ♕g6 17 ♕xb7 ♗c6 18
♕c7+! White wins) 13 ♕d5+
♔g6 14 ♗f4! ♖d8 15 ♖ad1
♖d7 16 ♖e3. The game Pinter
- Szell, Hungary 1971 continued 16 ... h6 17 ♖d4! ♔h7

18 ♗e5 ♕f7 19 ♕xb5 ♖g8 20
c4 g5 21 b4 a6 22 ♕c5 and
White soon won.
11   ♕h5+   g6
12   ♕e5+   ♔f7
13   ♕xh8
13 ♕d5+ is a mistake on
account of 13 ... ♔g7! 14
♕xe4 ♗xd6 and if 13 ♕xe4
then 13 ... ♗xd6 and Black
beats off the attack, re-
maining with an extra piece.

13   ...   ♘f6!
This, the suggestion of
Kurt Bardeleben ensures
Black the advantage in all
variations. Others are less
impressive, e.g.
a) **13 ... ♕d6** 14 ♕xh7+ ♗g7
15 ♗h6 ♕f8 (15 ... ♕f6 16
♖fe1 ♘g5 and now White
gest the advantage with 17
♖e7+! ♔xe7 18 ♗xg5 ♕xg5 19
♕xg7+) 16 ♖ad1 ♘f6 (noth-
ing else is satisfactory
either, e.g. 16 ... ♗g4 17 f3;.
16 ... ♗f5 17 g4!; 16 ... ♗e6 17

♖fe1) 17 ♕xg7+ ♕xg7 18 ♗xg7 ♔xg7 19 ♖d8! b6 20 ♖fd1 ♔f7 21 f3+- Karlsson - Jansson, Uppsala 1971.

b) **13 ... ♕f6!?** 14 ♕xh7+ ♔g7 15 ♗h6 and White has reasonable chances.

14 ♗g5

14 ♗h6 ♗e6 15 ♕xf8+ ♕xf8 16 ♗xf8 ♖xf8 17 ♖ad1 ♖d8 and White loses a pawn.

14 ...   ♗e6

Gipslis recommends **14 ... ♗f5** 15 ♖ad1 ♗g7.

15 ♖ad1

After 15 ♗xf6 ♕xf6 16 ♕xh7+ ♔g7 and 17 ... ♖h8, White loses the queen.

15 ...   ♗g7
16 ♕xd8   ♖xd8
17 ♖fe1

Mallée - Parma, Mannheim 1975. Now the simplest for Black was

17 ...   ♗f8!
18 ♗f4   ♘d5

With a winning position for Black (B. Parma)

B2

10 ♕d4

see following diagram

10 ...   ♘xe4

Also seen here is **10 ... ♗e7** 11 ♗g5! (the alternative

11 ♗f4 is weaker, e.g. 11 ... 0-0 and now 12 0-0-0 (12 ♕e5 ♖e8! 13 0-0-0 ♗f8 14 ♘xf6+ gxf6∓ Honos - Horvath, Hungary 1976) 12 ... ♘xe4 13 ♕xe4 ♖xf4! 14 ♕xe7 (14 dxe7 ♕xd1+ 15 ♔xd1 ♖xe4) 14 ... ♗d7 15 f3 ♖c8 16 ♖he1 ♖fc4 17 c3 b4 18 ♖e4 ♖xe4 19 fxe4 bxc3 20 ♕xd8+ ♖xd8 21 bxc3 ♔f7-+ Buiakovich - Mik. Tseitlin, Moscow 1989) when Black has two ways to play:

a) **11 ... ♗f5** 12 0-0-0 (12 ♘g3? ♗xc2 13 ♕d2 ♗xd6! 14 ♕xc2 ♗b4+∓) 12 ... ♗xe4 13 ♖he1 ♕xd6 (13 ... 0-0 14 dxe7 ♕xe7 15 ♗xf6 ♕xf6=) 14 ♕xd6 ♗xd6 15 ♖xd6 0-0 16 ♗xf6 ♗xg2 and a draw followed quickly in Halifman - Glek, Leningrad 1985.

b) **11 ... h6** 12 ♗h4 ♗f5 (Gipslis offers 12 ... g5 13 ♗g3 ♗f5 14 ♘c3 ♔f7 15 0-0-0 ♗f8 as a double-edged continuation) 13 0-0-0 (Diaz - Rodriguez, Havana 1982) 13 ... g5! 14 ♖he1 ♔f7 15 ♘xg5+! (according to Rodriguez, after 15 ♘g3 ♗xd6! 16 ♘xf5 ♗f4+ 17 ♔b1 ♕xd4 18 ♖xd4 ♖ae8 White cannot avoid material losses) 15 ... hxg5 16 ♖xe7+ ♔g6 (not 16 ... ♕xe7? 17 dxe7 gxh4 18 ♕e5±) 17 ♗xg5 ♔xg5 18 ♕e3+ with an attack sufficient for equality.

11   ♕xe4+   ♔f7
12   ♗f4

12 ♕d5+ ♗e6 (if 12 ... ♔g6 13 g4 is unpleasant) 13 ♕xb7+ ♔g8 (13 ... ♔g6 14 h4 h5! 15 ♗g5 ♕a5+ 16 ♗d2 ♕d8 17 ♗g5=) 14 ♗f4 ♖b8 15 ♕e4 ♕d7 16 0-0= Zuidema - van Schuur, Siegen 1970.

12   ...   ♕e8
13   ♗e5   ♗xd6

Belousov - Meshkov, 1978 saw 13 ... ♕c6 14 ♕f4+ ♔g8 15 0-0 (better 15 0-0-0!) and after 15 ... h5 16 ♖ad1 ♖h6 17 ♕g5 ♗d7 Black had a comfortable extra piece.

see following diagram

14   ♕d5+

14 ♕f3+ ♔e6! 15 0-0-0 ♗xe5 16 ♖he1 ♖f8∓

14   ...   ♕e6

15   ♕xd6   ♕xd6
16   ♗xd6   ♖e8+
17   ♔f1   ♗f5

Gonzales - Montalvo, Cuba 1978. Despite the pawn deficit, the endgame is favourable for Black.

B3

10   ♗g5

This modern continuation is the strongest.

10   ...   ♕a5+

Unimpressive is 10 ... ♗f5 11 ♗xf6 gxf6 12 ♕h5+ ♗g6 13 ♕xb5+ ♔f7 14 ♕xb7++- as mentioned by Bardeleben in 1904 and seen in the game Robatsch - Contendini, Leipzig 1960.

11 ♘c3!

This move breathes new life into the variation. Weaker is 11 ♗d2 b4 12 ♕e2 (12 ♘xf6+ gxf6 13 0-0, Grimmenshtein - Bardeleben, Berlin 1904 and now with 13 ... ♗d7! 14 ♖e1+ ♔f7 15 a3 ♗c6 16 ♗xb4 ♕g5 Black would get the advantage) 12 ... ♕e5 13 ♘xf6+ gxf6 14 ♕xe5+ fxe5 15 ♗xb4 ♖g8 16 0-0-0 (little better is 16 ♖d1 ♖g4! 17 ♗a3 ♖e4+ 18 ♔f1 ♗d7-+ Barry - Marshall, Cambridge Springs 1904) 16 ... ♗h6+ 17 ♗d2 ♗xd2+ 18 ♖xd2 ♖xg2 19 ♖e1 ♗e6 20 f4 ♖xd2 21 ♔xd2 e4! 22 ♖xe4 ♔d7 and Black soon won, Banas - Tatai, Stip 1979.

11 ... b4

11 ... ♗d7 12 ♗xf6 gxf6 13 ♕h5+ ♔d8 14 ♕f7 ♗xd6 15 0-0-0±

11 ... ♗e6 12 ♕e2 ♔d7 13 0-0 b4 14 ♗xf6! bxc3 15 ♗xc3 ♕f5 16 ♗e5±

In the latter variation, 12 ♗xf6!? was seen in Bushuiev - Chudakov, 1983. The continuation was 12 ... gxf6 13 ♕h5+ ♔d7 (13 ... ♗f7 14

d7+ ♔e7 15 ♕e2+ keeps the attack going) 14 0-0-0 ♖c8 15 ♖he1 ♖xc3 16 ♖xe6! ♗h6+ 17 ♕xh6! ♖xc2+ 18 ♔xc2 ♕a4+ 19 ♔d2 ♕b4+ 20 ♔e2+-

12 ♗xf6 gxf6

13 ♘d5

Not 13 0-0 bxc3 14 ♖e1+ ♔d8 and Black is defending.

13 ... b3+

13 ... ♗e6 14 ♕h5+ (14 ♘c7+ ♔f7 15 ♘xa8 ♕e5+ 16 ♕e2 ♗xd6∓) 14 ... ♔d8 15 0-0-0 b3! (much weaker is 15 ... ♖g8?! 16 d7!! ♗d6 17 ♖he1 ♗e5 18 ♖xe5 fxe5 19 ♕h4+ ♔xd7 20 ♕e7+ ♔c6 21 ♕xe6+ ♔b5 22 ♘c3+ 1 : 0 Glek - Jandemirov, 1983) 16 cxb3 (16 axb3 ♗xd5 {16 ... ♕a1+ 17 ♔d2 ♕xb2= or 17 ... ♕a5+=} 17 ♖xd5 ♕a1+ {not 17 ... ♗h6+? 18 ♔b1} 18 ♔d2 ♕xh1 19 ♕f7 ♖c8 leads to a draw) 16 ... ♖c8+ 17 ♔b1 ♖c5 18 ♕h4! (18 d7 ♗e7 and 18

b4 ♗xd5 19 bxa5 ♗e4+ are unacceptable for White) 18 ... ♗xd5 19 ♕xf6+ ♔d7 20 ♖xd5! ♖xd5 21 ♕xh8=

Returning to the diagram position, Piskov – Jandemirov, 1984 now continued ...

14	c3	♗e6!
15	♘c7+	♔d7
16	0–0	♗xd6
17	♘xe6	♕e5!
18	g3	♕xe6
19	♖e1?!	♕f7

20	axb3	♖he8!?
21	♖xe8	

And now with 21 ... ♖xe8! 22 ♖xa7 ♔c7 23 b4 ♕e6 Black would have got a definite advantage.

Instead of the inaccurate 19 ♖e1, **19 axb3** ♔c7 (19 ... ♖he8!?) 20 ♖e1 (20 b4!?) 20 ... ♕f7 21 ♕d4 should have been tried when White still preserves some counterchances.

5) 4 ♘c3 ♘f6 and 4 ... Others

1	e4	e5
2	♘f3	♘c6
3	♗b5	f5
4	♘c3	

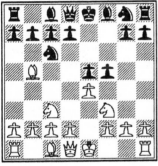

It should not be difficult to convince the reader that all the previous variations presented few problems for Black in obtaining good play. The move 4 ♘c3 is the most common response to 3 ... f5 and the one that presents Black with the most difficulties. The remaining chapters of this book are concerned with

play after this move.

In this chapter, we specifically consider the reply 4 ... ♘f6. The sixth chapter deals with 4 ... ♘d4 and the final three with the most popular continuation, 4 ... fxe4 5 ♘xe4.

4 ... ♘f6 is an interesting way for Black to try to steer clear of the heavy theory associated with some variations beginning with 4 ... dxe4. Black maintains flexibility whilst increasing the pressure against White's centre. The drawback is that White can consider the capture exf5, either immediately or in the near future, attempting to play a 'King's Gambit Accepted' strategy. The 4 ... ♘f6 variation almost always involves the sacrifice of a pawn for the initiative, but if Black players were

afraid to follow such a strategy, they would be unlikely to be playing the Schliemann in the first place!

Other possibilities for Black on the fourth move:

4 ... ♗c5 proves unsatisfactory following 5 0-0 ♘f6 6 ♘xe5! 0-0 7 ♗c4+ d5 8 ♘xd5 ♘xe5 9 ♘xf6+ ♔h8 10 ♘xh7 ♘xc4 11 ♕h5 ♕e8 12 ♕h4 ♔g8 13 ♘g5 ♕g6 14 exf5 ♖xf5 15 ♕xc4+ ♔h8 16 d4+- Karajants – Dobrojevic, Belgrade 1956.

Kaiser's move, **4 ... ♗b4!?** is more deserving of attention, e.g.

a) **5 ♘d5?** fxe4 6 ♘xb4 exf3 7 ♗xc6 bxc6 8 ♕xf3 ♘f6 9 0-0 0-0 10 a4 a5∓ Sundstrom – Kaiser, Stockholm 1947.

b) **5 d3** fxe4 6 dxe4 ♘f6 is a position that was examined in chapter three.

c) **5 ♕e2** ♗xc3 6 dxc3 d6 7 exf5 ♗xf5 8 ♗g5 ♘f6 9 0-0-0 ♕e7! 10 ♕c4 ♗d7 11 ♖he1 h6! 12 ♗h4 0-0-0 13 ♘d4 (Skold – Kaiser, Stockholm 1951) 13 ... ♘b8! with a complex game.

d) **5 exf5!** ♘ge7!? 6 f6! (not 6 d4? e4 7 ♘g5 ♘xf5 8 d5 e3! 9 dxc6 bxc6 10 ♗xc6 (10 ♘e6 ♕f6!) 10 ... ♕f6 11 ♗xa8 ♗xc3+-+, Kaiser) 6 ... gxf6 7 d4±

4 ...   ♘f6

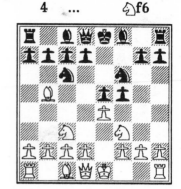

Now we consider:

A) 5 ♕e2
B) 5 exf5

Others are harmless:

a) **5 ♗xc6** bxc6 6 ♕e2 (6 ♘xe5 ♗a6) 6 ... d5 7 exf5 ♗d6 8 ♘xe5 0-0 9 ♘xc6 ♕d7 10 ♕e6+ ♔h8 11 ♕xd7 ♗xd7∓ Lublinski – Stein, Moscow 1955.

b) **5 d4** exd4 (5 ... fxe4 6 ♘xe5 ♗b4 is also possible) 6 ♘xd4 fxe4 7 0-0 ♘xd4 8 ♕xd4 c6 9 ♘xe4 ♘xe4 10 ♕xe4+ ♕e7, and after the exchange of queens the chances will be about equal. Instead in Bilek – Barcza, Budapest 1954, White decided to sacrifice a piece with 11 ♕f3? but after 11 ... cxb5 12 ♗f4 d5 13 ♖fe1 ♗e6 had insufficient compensation.

A

5 ♕e2

Here two responses are possible:

A1) 5 ... ♘d4
A2) 5 ... ♗c5

A1

5 ... ♘d4

Marshall's pet variation, which he successfully employed in his match against Capablanca (New York, 1909).

6 ♘xd4 exd4

7 exf5+

7 ♘d5 ♘xd5 8 exd5+ ♕e7 9 0-0 ♕xe2 10 ♗xe2 ♗e7 "=" (ECO)

7 **e5** leads to interesting complications after 7 ... ♘g4 8 h3 ♘h6. Teichmann

- Marshall, Monte Carlo 1903 went 9 ♘b1 (9 ♘d1 ♕e7 (9 ... ♕g5!?) 10 c3 c6 11 ♗d3 (11 ♗c4 also failed to pose Black any problems in Grunfeld - Rodriguez, New York Open 1987. Following 11 ... d5 12 exd6 ♕xe2+ 13 ♔xe2 ♘f7 14 ♖e1 ♘xd6 15 ♔f1+ ♗e7 16 d3 ♘xc4 17 dxc4 ♔f7 18 cxd4 ♗f6 19 d5 cxd5 20 cxd5 ♖d8 21 ♘c3 b5 22 a3 ♗b7 23 ♗e3 the game was agreed drawn) 11 ... dxc3 (11 ... d5!? 12 cxd4 ♕b4 13 ♕e3 g5!) 12 dxc3 ♘f7 13 ♗xf5 (13 0-0 d6) 13 ... ♕xe5= Spassky - Bisguier, Goteborg 1955) 9 ... ♕g5 10 0-0 c6 11 ♗c4 f4 12 d3 d5! 13 exd6+ ♔d8! 14 ♘d2! ♗xh3 15 ♕f3 ♗f5 16 ♘e4 ♗xe4 17 dxe4 ♗xd6 18 c3 d3! with a balanced position.

7	...	♗e7
8	♘e4!	0-0
9	♘xf6+	♗xf6
10	0-0	d5

see following diagram

This variation was tested out in the Capablanca - Marshall match mentioned above.

11 ♕h5

11 ♗d3 is inferior to the text, e.g. 11 ... c5 12 ♕h5

♛e7 13 c4! dxc4 14 ♗xc4+
♚h8 15 d3 ♛e5 16 g4 ♗d7 17
a4 was the second match
game. Now with 17 ... ♗c6
or 17 ... ♛e2, Marshall
could have obtained good
play.

11   ...   c5

11 ... ♗e5 12 ♘d3 ♖f6 in-
tending to swing the rook
is worth consideration.

12   ♘e2   ♖e8

12 ... ♗e5 13 g4 d3! 14
♗xd3 ♖f6, and 12 ... ♛e8 13
♛f3 ♛e5 14 g4 ♗d8 also
offer good chances for
Black.

13   ♗g4   d3!
14   cxd3   b6∓

Capablanca - Marshall,
also from their New York
1909 match (10th game).
Black clearly has the more
comfortable position.

A2

5   ♛e2   ♗c5

6   exf5

6 d3 ♘d4 7 ♘xd4 ♗xd4 8
♗c4 f4 9 g3 f3! 10 ♛xf3 d5 11
exd5 0-0 12 ♛e2 ♗g4 13 f3
♘e4! with strong threats
for Black, Wolf - Nimzo-
witsch, Berlin 1905.

6   ...   ♛e7
7   d3

Taking the second pawn
doesn't lead anywhere for
White, e.g. 7 ♗xc6 dxc6 8
♛xe5 ♗xf2+ (8 ... ♛xe5+ 9
♘xe5 ♗xf5 10 d3 0-0 11 0-0
♖ae8 12 ♘c4 ♘g4 and the
active Black pieces fully
compensate for the missing
pawn, Bertok - Fuderer,
Ljubliana 1951) 9 ♚e2 ♛xe5+
10 ♘xe5 ♗d4 11 ♘f3 ♗xc3 12
bxc3 ♗xf5= Witkowski -
Barcza, Prague 1955.

7 ♘e4 ♘xe4 8 ♛xe4 0-0 9
0-0 d6! 10 ♗xc6 bxc6 11 d4
(11 ♛xc6 ♗xf5 12 d3 ♖ab8
b3) 11 ... ♗xf5 12 ♛e2 ♗b6 13
dxe5 d5 with an active pos-

ition, Bagirov - Holmov, Moscow 1961.

	7	...	♘d4
	8	♘xd4	♗xd4

Here Black has sufficient compensation for the pawn.

9 0-0

9 ♗e3 c6 10 ♗a4 ♗xc3+! 11 bxc3 d6 12 0-0 ♗xf5 13 ♖ab1 0-0 14 c4 ♗g6∓ Ravinsky – Soloviev, Moscow 1955.

	9	...	c6
	10	♗a4	d5

10 ... d6 11 ♕f3 ♗d7 12 ♘e2 ♗b6 13 ♘g3 0-0-0 14 ♗g5 h6! 15 ♗h4 ♖df8 16 ♖fe1 (16 ♘h5 ♕f7 17 ♘xf6 gxf6) 16 ... g5! 17 fxg6 ♕g7 with a dangerous attack, Bardeleben - Duz-Hotimirsky, Prague 1908.

	11	♗g5	0-0
	12	♗b3	♗xf5

Black has a typically good attacking position, Chalkhasuren - Boey, Varna 1962

B

5 exf5

This is a position from the King's Gambit Declined with colours reversed. White hopes that the extra tempo (♗b5) will lead to an advantage, but things are not so simple. Let us consider Black's responses:

B1) 5 ... e4
B2) 5 ... ♗c5
B3) 5 ... ♘d4

Others:

a) 5 ... ♗e7 6 d4 (6 ♗xc6 dxc6 7 ♘xe5 0-0 8 0-0 ♗xf5 with an active position) 6 ... exd4 7 ♘xd4 ♘xd4 8 ♕xd4 0-0 9 0-0 d5 10 ♗g5 ♗xf5 11 ♗xf6 ♗xf6 12 ♕xd5+ ♕xd5 13 ♘xd5 ♗xb2= Leonhardt - Marshall, Cologne 1911.

b) 5 ... ♗b4 6 0-0 (6 ♗xc6 dxc6 7 ♘xe5!?) 6 ... 0-0 7 d4 e4 8 ♘e5 (8 ♘h4 d5 9 g4

♘xg4!? 10 ♕xg4 ♘xd4 11 ♗g5 ♗e7 12 ♗xe7 ♕xe7 13 ♔h1 c6 14 ♗e2 ♘xc2 15 ♖ad1 ♕e5 16 ♖g1 ♗xf5! 17 ♘xf5 ♖xf5 18 ♘xd5 ♖xf2 Maistrovich - Liublinski, Correspondence 1975) 8 ... ♕e8! 9 ♕e2 ♗xc3 10 ♕c4+ d5 11 ♕xc3 ♘xd4! 12 ♗xe8 ♘e2+ 13 ♔h1 ♘xc3 14 ♗f7+ ♖xf7 15 ♘xf7 ♔xf7 16 bxc3 ♗xf5 17 ♗e3 b6 18 ♖fd1 (better is 18 h3) 18 ... ♔e6 19 a4 a5 20 ♗f4 ♖c8 21 c4 dxc4 22 ♖d4 ♘d5 23 ♗e3 c3 24 h3 h5 25 ♔h2 ♔e5∓ Ekstrom - Liublinski, Correspondence 1975

B1
5   ...   e4

This old continuation is viewed by theory as being to White's advantage, although in our estimation there are insufficient grounds for this assessment.

6   ♘g5

Considered the strongest. In Pillsbury - Tarrasch, Monte Carlo 1903, White played weakly: **6 ♕e2 ♕e7 7 ♗xc6 bxc6 8 ♘h4 d5 9 d4 a5∓**.

6 ♘h4 is an interesting possibility, insisting on holding on to the gambit pawn in a most direct fashion. Some old analysis by

Lasker goes 6 ... ♘d4 7 ♗e2 (or 7 d3 c6! 8 ♗a4 d5 9 dxe4 dxe4 10 ♗g5 ♗b4 11 0-0 ♗xc3 12 bxc3 ♘xf5=) 7 ... ♘xe2 8 ♕xe2 d5 9 d3 ♗b4=. However, the only outing with 6 ♘h4 to date, resulted in a singular success for White after 7 ♗a4!? ♗c5 8 d3 b5 (Black is trying to exploit White's 7th move, but his aggressive play backfires when he overlooks White's cunning tactical ploy on move 12) 9 ♗b3 exd3 10 ♕xd3 ♕e7+ 11 ♗e3 ♘g4 12 f6! gxf6 13 ♘d5 ♘e5 14 ♕d1 1-0 Georgiev - Rodriguez, Terrassa 1990. 7 ♗a4!? is fertile territory for further research.

6 ... d5 (after 6 ♘h4) is also possible

Practice demonstrates that Black has sufficient compensation:

a) **7 g4 ♘d7! 8 ♘g2** (8

♘xd5 ♕xh4 9 ♘xc7+ ♔e7 10 ♘xa8 ♘d4 11 ♗e2 ♘e5-+) 8 ... ♘d4 9 d3 c6 10 ♗a4 exd3 11 ♕xd3 ♘e5∓ Suchting - Teichmann, Vienna 1908.

b) **7 d3 ♗e7** (after 7 ... d4 Lasker recommends 8 ♘xe4 {8 ♘b1 exd3 9 ♕xd3 ♕e7+ 10 ♕e2 [10 ♔d1 ♘e4] 10 ... ♗d7 11 ♗g5 0-0-0 12 ♘d2 ♖e8!∓ Janowski - Marshall, match 1905} 8 ... ♘xe4 9 ♕h5+ g6 10 ♘xg6 ♘f6 11 ♕e2+ ♔f7 12 ♘xh8+ ♔g8 with a double-edged position) 8 dxe4 dxe4 9 ♕xd8+ ♗xd8 10 ♗g5 0-0= Capablanca - Marshall, match, New York 1909.

c) **7 d4 ♗e7** 8 g4 0-0 (8 ... g5!? 9 ♗xg5 ♖g8) 9 ♗xc6? (9 ♖g1 as in the analogous King's Gambit position) 9 ... bxc6 10 ♘g2 ♗a6 11 ♗g5 ♖b8 12 ♖b1 c5∓ Rosenfeld - Marshall, New York 1910.

Returning to the position after 6 ♘g5

6 ... d5

6 ... ♘d4 7 ♗a4 c6 8 d3 and Black obtained no compensation in Aronin - Klaman, Leningrad 1947.

7 d3   ♗xf5

7 ... h6 8 ♘e6 ♗xe6 9 fxe6 ♕d6 10 dxe4 d4 (no better is 10 ... ♕xe6 11 0-0! dxe4 12 ♗f4 ♗d6 13 ♗xd6! cxd6 14 ♕e2 (14 f3!?) 14 ... d5 15 ♖ad1± Yudakov - Goliakberov, Talgari 1977) 11 ♗xc6+ bxc6 12 ♘e2 0-0-0 13 ♕d3! c5 14 f3 ♕xe6 15 ♘f4 ♕c6 16 b3 ♗d6 17 ♘e2 ♖de8 (better is 17 ... ♖he8) 18 0-0 g5 19 c3!± Yershov - Glazkov, Kuibyshev 1953.

8 dxe4   dxe4
9 ♕e2

9 ♗xc6+ bxc6 10 ♕e2 ♗b4 11 ♗d2 (11 ♕c4 ♗xc3+) 11 ... ♗xc3 12 ♗xc3 0-0 13 0-0 ♕d5 and with ... ♕b5 coming up, Black is okay.

9 0-0 h6! 10 ♘gxe4 ♘xe4 11 ♘xe4 ♕xd1 12 ♖xd1 ♗xe4 13 ♖e1 0-0-0 14 ♖xe4 ♖d1+ 15 ♗f1 ♗c5-+

9 ...   ♕d7!

F. Marshall's forgotten recommendation. With this move Black can consolidate.

9 ... ♗b4 10 ♗d2 ♕e7 11 ♕c4 ♖d8 12 ♗xc6+ bxc6 13 0-0-0± was Leonhardt - Spielmann, Nuremburg 1906

and also unsatisfactory was **9 ... ♗d6** 10 ♗xc6+ bxc6 11 ♕c4 ♔d7 12 ♗e3 ♕g8 13 ♕a4 and Black has no compensation for the numerous weaknesses.

10   ♘gxe4   0-0-0

In this critical position Black has satisfactory play.

11   ♗g5

Probably better is **11 0-0** ♘xe4 12 ♘xe4 ♖e8 13 f3 ♗xe4 14 fxe4 ♕d4+ which is approximately equal.

11	...	♘xe4!
12	♘xe4	♗xe4!
13	♗xd8	♗xg2
14	♖g1	♗b4+∓

B2)

5   ...   ♗c5

This was first used in the game Bardeleben - Duz-Hotimirsky, Prague 1908, and was then forgotten about for nearly fifty years!

6   0-0

6 ♗xc6 is a mistake, e.g. 6 ... dxc6 7 ♘xe5 (7 ♘a4 ♗xf2+ 8 ♔xf2 e4) 7 ... ♗xf2+ 8 ♔xf2 ♕d4+ 9 ♔f3 ♗xf5 10 ♖e1 0-0-+

6 ♘xe5 ♘d4 (6 ... 0-0 7 ♘f3! d5 (7 ... ♖e8+ 8 ♗e2) 8 d4 ♗b6 9 0-0 ♗xf5 10 h3±, Euwe) 7 0-0 0-0 leads to the main continuation.

6 d3!? 0-0 7 ♘e4 ♗e7 8 ♘g3 ♘d4 9 ♘xd4 exd4 10 0-0 c6 11 ♗a4 d5 12 ♗f4 ♗d6 13 ♕d2 ♕c7 14 ♗xd6 ♕xd6 15 ♗b3 ♔h8 16 ♖ae1 ♗d7 17 ♖e2 ♘g4 18 ♕g5 ♘h6 19 ♖e7 ♘f7 20 ♕h4 ♘h6 21 ♖fe1 ♘f5 22 ♘xf5 ♖xf5 23 ♕g3 1-0 (as after 23 ... ♕xg3 24 hxg3, Black is in a tangle on the back rank and must lose a piece) was van Riemsdijk - Klip Dieren Open 1989. Black's 7 ... ♗e7 looks rather passive. 7 ... ♗b6 maintaining the strong diagonal for black bishop looks more to the point.

6 ... 0-0

7 ♘xe5

Practice demonstrates that White has little chance of an advantage with other moves:

a) 7 ♗xc6 dxc6 8 ♘xe5 ♗xf5 9 ♘c4 (9 d3 ♕e8 10 ♕e2 ♗d4 11 ♖e1 ♘g4 led to a promising endgame for Black in Magem - Rodriguez, Terrassa 1990. Play continued 12 ♘xg4 ♗xg4 13 ♕xe8 ♗xf2+ 14 ♔h1 ♖axe8 15 ♖xe8 ♖xe8 16 ♗f4 ♗d4 17 h3 ♗h5 18 ♗xc7 ♗xc3 19 bxc3 ♖e2 20 ♖b1 b5 21 a4 a6 22 axb5 axb5 23 c4 bxc4 24 dxc4 ♗g6 25 ♔g1 ♗e4 26 g3 g5 with a pleasant initiative for Black, although he went on to lose) 9 ... ♘g4 10 ♘e3 ♕h4 11 h3 ♘xe3 12 dxe3 ♗xh3 13 gxh3 ♖f6 14 ♔g2 ♖g6+ 0 : 1 Kuznetsova - Kantorovich, Moscow 1961.

b) 7 ♖e1 d6 8 ♘a4 (better is 8 d3) 8 ... e4! 9 ♘xc5 dxc5 10 ♗xc6 bxc6 11 ♘h4 g5! 12 fxg6 ♘g4∓ Matanovic - Janosevic, Belgrade 1958.

c) 7 ♘a4 ♗e7 8 d4 ♘xd4 9 ♘xd4 exd4 10 ♕xd4 c5!? 11 ♘xc5 ♕b6 12 ♗c4+ d5 13 ♗xd5+ ♔h8 14 ♗e3 ♘xd5 15 ♕xd5 ♖xf5 16 ♕e4 ♗xc5 17 ♕e8+ ♖f8 18 ♕xf8+ ♗xf8 19 ♗xb6 axb6 20 ♖fe1 Zelevinsky - Selivanovsky, Moscow 1957, and now with 20 ... ♗d7, Black's bishop pair would give him excellent prospects.

7 ... ♘d4

The continuation 7 ... ♘xe5 8 d4 ♗xd4 9 ♕xd4 d6 is dubious, e.g. 10 ♗f4! ♗xf5 11 ♗xe5 dxe5 12 ♕xe5 ♗xc2 13 ♗c4+! ♔h8 14 ♘b5± Stein - Nadezhdin, 1962.

Now:

B21) 8 ♗a4
B22) 8 ♘f3

Others:

a) 8 ♘d3 ♗b6 9 ♘f4 d5 10 d3 ♗xf5 11 ♗e3 c6 12 ♗a4 ♘g4∓

b) 8 ♗e2 d5 9 ♘f3 ♗xf5 (9 ... ♘xe2+ 10 ♘xe2 ♗xf5) 10

♘xd4 ♗xd4 11 d3 ♗e5 12 d4
♗d6 13 ♘b5 ♗e7∞

B21
    8 ♗a4
This bishop retreat is a
loss of time and allows
Black to develop a dangerous initiative.
    8 ... d5

Here there is a further
dichotomy:

B211) 9 ♘e2
B212) 9 ♘f3

    9 ♘b5?! ♗xf5 10 c3 ♘xb5
11 ♗xb5 d4 12 ♕b3+ ♔h8 13
♗d3 (13 ♘f7+ ♖xf7 14 ♕xf7
d3) 13 ... ♘g4 14 ♗xf5 ♘xe5
15 ♗h3 ♘d3 16 ♕c4 dxc3 17
dxc3 ♖xf2-+ Lukov - Inkiov,
Pamporovo 1982.

B211
    9 ♘e2
This move, which was
considered the strongest,
has been re-assessed.

see following diagram

    9 ... ♕d6!
An excellent reply, found
by Rodriguez. Previously
9 ... ♕e7 had been played
when, although 10 ♘xd4

♕xe5 11 ♘e2 ♘g4 12 g3
♘xf2! 13 ♖xf2 ♗xf5 gives
Black a very dangerous
attack, White can improve
with 11 ♘f3!, e.g. 11 ... ♕xf5
12 d4 ♗d6 13 c3 ♘e4 14 ♗e3
Zurachov - Zaitsev, Leningrad 1963. Now with 14 ...
♕f6 Black might just about
maintain the balance.
    10 ♘xd4
    10 ♘d3 ♗b6 11 ♘xd4 (11
♘g3 ♘xf5) 11 ... ♗xd4∞
    10 ... ♗xd4
    11 ♘f3
    11 ♘g4? fails to 11 ...
♘xg4 12 ♕xg4 ♕b4! Hulak
- Rodriguez, Karlovec 1979.
    11 ... ♘g4
    12 c3
Other White tries:
    a) **12 h3** ♗xf5 13 d3 (13 c3
♗e4 14 hxg4 ♗xf3) 13 ...
♘xf2 (also good is 13 ... ♗e6
△ ♖xf3) 14 ♖xf2 ♗xf2+ 15
♔xf2 ♗xh3!-+
    b) **12 g3** ♗xf2+ 13 ♖xf2

♘xf2 14 ♔xf2 ♗xf5 15 d4 (15 d3 ♗g4 16 ♘f4 ♖xf4! 17 gxf4 ♕xf4) 15 ... ♗e4 16 ♘f4 ♖xf4! 17 gxf4 ♕xf4 18 ♕e2 ♖f8∓ Marjanovic - Parma, Yugoslavia 1979.

c) **12 ♕e2 ♗xf5 13 ♕b5 ♗e6! 14 ♕xb7 ♖xf3! 15 ♕xa8+ ♖f8 16 ♕xf8+ ♕xf8** 0 : 1 Emelin - Rozumenko, Correspondence 1983.

12 ...   ♖xf5
13 cxd4

13 g3 is no good in view of 13 ... ♗xf2+! 14 ♖xf2 ♘xf2 15 ♔xf2 ♖f6 16 d4 ♗g4 17 ♘f4 ♖xf4 18 gxf4 ♕xf4.

13 h3 ♖xf3 14 hxg4 ♗xg4 (also 14 ... ♖h3 15 gxh3 ♕g3+ 16 ♔h1 ♕xh3+ is very good) 15 ♕e1 ♖h3!! and Black won, Gonsher - Freize, 1979.

13 ...   ♖xf3
14 g3   ♘xh2
Nikitin suggests 14 ... ♕h6 15 h4 ♖f6 or 15 ... ♖d3 as being to Black's advantage. Black can also try 14 ... ♖xf2 15 ♖xf2 ♘xf2 16 ♔xf2 ♗h3! 17 d3 (17 ♔g1 ♕f6 {17 ... ♖f8 18 d3 ♕b4}) 17 ... ♖f8+ 18 ♘f4 ♕b4! 19 ♔g1 ♕xd4+ 20 ♔h1 ♕xb2 21 ♕g1 ♗g2+ 22 ♕xg2 ♕xa1+ 23 ♕g1 ♕xa2-+ Tatai and Zinser.

15 ♔xh2   ♕h6+
16 ♔g1

If **16 ♔g2 ♗h3+ 17 ♔xf3** then 17 ... ♕e6!-+
16 ...   ♗g4
17 ♕e1
After **17 d3 ♕h3 18 ♕e1** the simplest is 18 ... ♖f5!
17 ...   ♕h3
Also very good is 17 ... ♖f5, e.g. 18 ♗d1 (18 d3 ♕h1+!) 18 ... ♖h5! 19 ♗xg4 ♖h1+ 20 ♔g2 ♕h2+ 21 ♔f3 ♖f8+ 22 ♘f5 (22 ♔e2 ♖e8+ 23 ♔d1 ♖xe1+ 24 ♔xe1 ♖xf1+ 25 ♔xf1 ♕h1+ 26 ♔e2 ♕e4+) 22 ... ♖xf5+ 23 ♔e2 ♕h5+ 24 f3 (24 ♔d3 ♖f3+ 25 ♔c2 ♕f5+ 26 ♔d1 ♖xf1 27 ♕xf1 ♖xf2) 24 ... ♖f6! 25 d3 ♖h2+ 26 ♔d1 ♕g6! 27 ♔c3 (27 ♗d2 ♕xd3) 27 ... ♕xg3 28 ♗d2 ♕g2 29 ♖e1 ♕xf3+ 30 ♔c2 ♖c6 31 ♖e8+ ♔f7 32 ♖ae1 ♕f2 0 : 1 Polgar - Morvay, Hungary 1982.

18 ♗d1   ♖af8
19 d3

19 ...   h6!

19 ... ♖xf2 allows White the possibility of an interesting defence – 20 ♕xf2! ♖xf2 21 ♔xf2! ♕h2+ 22 ♔e1! ♕xg3+ 23 ♖f2 ♕g1+ and Black must take a draw (23 ... ♗xd1 24 ♗f4⩲)

| 20 | ♗f4 | ♖8xf4! |

Not **20 ...** ♖f5? in view of 21 ♕e6+ ♔h7 22 ♕xf5+!

21	gxf4	♗h5
22	♕e3	♖xe3
23	fxe3	♕xe3+
24	♔h1	♗g6
25	♗f3	♕xd4
26	b3	♗xd3
27	♖ad1	c6
28	♗g2	c5
29	♔h2	c4
30	bxc4	dxc4

0 : 1

Votea – Lukacs, Correspondence 1975/76.

B212

| 9 | ♘f3 | ♗xf5 |
| 10 | ♘xd4 | ♗xd4 |

11 ♘e2

By removing the dangerous knight on d4, White can hope for a successful defence. Too risky is **11 d3?** ♘g4! when Black develops a dangerous initiative, e.g.

a) **12 g3** ♘e5! 13 ♘e2 ♗g4! 14 c3 ♗f3!! and White is defenceless against the terrible threat of ♕d8 – c8 – h3.

b) **12 ♗f4** ♘xf2! 13 ♖xf2 ♗xf2+ 14 ♔xf2 ♕h4+ 15 ♗g3 ♕d4+ 16 ♔e1 ♗g4 0 : 1 Lombard – Jansen, The Hague 1967.

c) **12 ♕f3** ♗e6 13 ♕e2 ♕h4! 14 ♕xe6+ ♔h8 15 h3 ♖xf2 16 ♗e3 ♖xf1+ 17 ♖xf1 ♘xe3 18 ♖b1 ♕g3! 0 : 1 Gerhard-Nielson, Correspondence 1979.

d) **12 ♕e2** ♕h4 13 ♗f4 ♘xf2 with a very strong attack, Mazian – Afek, Israel 1980.

| 11 | ... | ♗g4 |
| 12 | c3 |

12 ♔h1 ♗xe2 (or 12 ... ♘e4 13 f3 ♕h4) 13 ♕xe2 ♘e4 14 f3 ♕h4! 15 fxe4 ♖xf1+ 16 ♕xf1 ♖f8–+

| 12 | ... | ♕e7! |
| 13 | ♗b5 |

13 ♕e1 ♗xe2 14 cxd4 ♔f7∓ Buljovcic – Bojkovic, Novi Sad 1979.

13   ...   ♖ae8

In Karpov - Hermann, Bad Lauterberg 1977 Black got carried away with **13 ... ♗xf2+?** and after **14 ♖xf2 ♕c5 15 ♕b3** White held off the attack while maintaining the extra piece.

13 ... a6 14 cxd4 (14 ♗d3 ♖ae8 is the main line) **14 ... axb5 15 f3 ♖ae8!** (Dorfman) and Black gets the advantage in all variations, e.g 16 ♖e1 ♗xf3! 17 gxf3 ♘h5 or 16 ♖f2 ♘e4! 17 ♘g3 (17 ♘c3 gets the same reply) 17 ... ♕b4!

14   cxd4

14 ♗xe8? ♗xe2.

14   ...   ♗xe2
15   ♗xe2   ♕xe2

In this critical position Black stands okay despite the pawn deficit.

16   d3   ♘h5!

Less incisive is **16 ... c6** 17 h3 ♘h5! 18 ♗e3 ♕xd1 19 ♖axd1 ♘g3! 20 ♖fe1 ♘f5= Stoica - Ciocaltea, Bucharest 1980.

17	**♕e3**	**♖xe3!**
18	**fxe3**	**♕xe3+**
19	**♔h1**	**♘g3+!**
20	**hxg3**	**♕h6+**
21	**♔g1**	**♕e3+**

With a draw by perpetual.

B22

8   ♘f3

This immediate attack on the centralised knight reduces Black's attacking possibilities.

8   ...   c6

The most common, but in our opinion not the best, reply. Preferable is **8 ... ♘xf5!** 9 d4 ♗b6. The game Bobotsov - Kostov, Sofia 1960 continued thus: 10 ♗g5 c6 11 ♗d3 d5 12 ♘e2 h6 13 ♗xf6 ♕xf6 14 c3 ♗c7 15 ♗c2 ♘h4 16 ♘xh4 ♕xh4 17 ♘g3 and now with 17 ... ♗g4! 18

♕d3 (18 ♕b1? ♗e2 19 ♖e1
♖ae8) 18 ... ♗f5 Black
would stand excellently.

Other plans fail to equalise for Black:

a) 8 ... ♘xf3+ 9 ♕xf3 d5.
Timman - Lombardy, Am-
sterdam 1974 continued 10
♗d3 c6 11 b3 ♘d7 12 ♕g3
♕f6 13 ♗b2 ♗d4 14 ♖ae1 ♘c5
15 ♗a3! ♘xd3 16 cxd3 ♗xf5
17 ♗xf8! ♖xf8 18 ♘e2 ♗b6 19
♘f4 ♗c7 20 ♘xd5±

b) 8 ... ♘xb5 9 ♘xb5 d5
10 ♘bd4. Smailbegovic -
Maric, Yugoslavia 1957 further saw 10 ... ♘g4 (10 ...
♕d6 11 d3 ♘g4 12 h3 ♘h2 13
♘b5 ♘xf3+ 14 ♕xf3 ♕d7 15
g4! ♗xf2+ 16 ♖xf2 ♕xb5 17
♗f4 ♗d7 18 c3 d4 19 c4 ♕c5
20 ♕xb7+- Vasiukov - Eg-
orov, Moscow 1959) 11 h3
♘e5 12 ♘xe5 ♗xd4 13 ♘f3
♗b6 and now for some
reason, White refrained
from 14 g4! which would
have maintained two extra
pawns.

White tried to improve
over this with 10 d4 in
Velimirovic - Terzic, Zenica
1987. However, White failed
to do justice to his idea, as
following 10 ... ♗b6 11 ♘e5
♗xf5 12 ♗e3 ♘d7 13 ♕d2
♕e8 he promptly blundered
a piece with 14 ♘c3?? Black

was alert to the tactics in
the position and after 14 ...
♘xe5 15 dxe5 d4! 16 ♗xd4
♖d8 17 ♘e2 ♗xd4 18 ♘xd4
c5 he went on to win easily.
White should, of course,
have played 14 ♘xd7 ♕xd7
when Black has the typical
compensation of the bishop
pair and open lines for his
pawn sacrifice.

c) 8 ... d5 9 ♘xd4 ♗xd4 10
♘e2 ♗b6 11 ♘g3 (11 d4) 11 ...
♘e4 12 ♘xe4 dxe4 13 ♗c4+
♔h8 14 ♗e6 ♗xe6 15 fxe6.
Arseniev - Kovalenko, Mo-
scow 1957 now saw 15 ...
♖xf2!? 16 ♖xf2 ♕f6 17 ♕e1
♖f8 18 d4! ♕xd4 19 e7! and
after 19 ... ♖e8 20 ♔f1 White
held off the attack, with a
big advantage. At first
sight, Black could have re-
solved the game in his favour with 19 ... ♖xf2, but
White has a beautiful re-
futation, e.g. 20 ♗e3!! (not
20 e8♕+? ♖f8+) 20 ... ♕xe3
21 ♕xe3 ♗xe3 22 ♔h1 and
the White pawn promotes.
19 ... ♕xf2+ doesn't help
Black - 20 ♕xf2 ♖xf2 21
♗e3 with the same conclu-
sion.

9 ♘xd4

In the correspondence
game Shapovalov - Zhurav-
lev, 1963 a recommendation

of Suetin was seen: **9 b4!?**
♘xf3+ 10 ♕xf3 ♗xb4 11 ♗d3
d5 12 ♗b2 ♘e8 13 ♖ae1 and
now after the error 13 ...
♕g5? White landed an un-
expected blow 14 ♘xd5!
cxd5 15 ♕xd5+ ♔h8 16 ♕b5
♗e7 17 f4±

9   ...   ♗xd4

10   ♗d3

10 ♗a4 d5 11 ♘e2 ♗b6 12
d4! ♗xf5 13 ♗f4! Unzicker
– Nievergelt, Zurich 1959
continued 13 ... ♘h5 (no
better is 13 ... ♕e8 14 ♗d6
♘g4 15 f3 ♕e3+ 16 ♔h1 ♖fe8
17 ♘g3 ♗d7 18 c3±) 14 ♗e5
♕h4 15 ♘g3 ♗g4 16 ♕d2±

13 ♘g3 should also be
good for White. Agnos –
Erker, Lloyds Bank 1988
continued 13 ... ♗g6 14 ♗f4
♘e4 15 ♗e5 ♕g5 16 f4 ♘xg3
and now with 17 fxg5 White
would have obtained a
small endgame advantage.
In the game, his attempt to

play for more with 17 ♖f3?
backfired horribly to the
tactical sequence 17 ...
♕xe5! 18 fxe5 ♗xd4+ 19
♕xd4 ♘e2+ 20 ♔h1 ♘xd4 21
♖xf8+ ♖xf8 22 c3 ♘e6 0–1.

10   ♗e2 (perhaps more
convincing than the text)
10 ... d5 11 ♗f3 (11 d3 ♗xf5 12
♗f4! ♕d7 13 ♕d2± Gligoric
– Matulovic, Yugoslavia
1957) 11 ... ♗xf5 12 ♘e2! ♗b6
13 d4± Vasilchuk – Stein,
Moscow 1956.

10	...	d5
11	♘e2	♗e5!
12	♘g3	♘e4!
13	♗xe4	dxe4
14	d3	exd3
15	♕xd3	♕xd3
16	cxd3	♗xg3
17	hxg3	♗xf5=

Tal – Spassky, Moscow
1957.

B3

5   ...   ♘d4

6 0-0

6 ♘xd4 exd4 7 ♘e2 c6 was Freize – Schuster, Neishtadt 1957, and Black obtained the advantage after 8 ♗d3 ♗c5 9 ♘g3 0-0 10 0-0 d5 11 ♕f3 ♕d6 12 c3 (12 b3 ♘d7) 12 ... ♗b6 13 ♘e2 ♘e4!∓

6 d3 is well met by 6 ... c6! 7 ♗a4 d5.

6 ♗a4 ♗c5 7 0-0 (if White chooses instead 7 d3 then as well as 7 ... 0-0 8 0-0 {8 ♘e4 ♘xe4 9 dxe4 d5} 8 ... d5, which is fine, Black can also consider 7 ... ♘xf5!?, e.g. 8 ♘e4 ♗b6 9 ♘xe5 0-0 10 0-0 d5 11 ♘xf6+ ♕xf6 12 ♘d7 ♗xd7 13 ♗xd7 ♖f7∞ Baikov – Mik. Tseitlin, Moscow 1979) 7 ... 0-0

Now:

a) **8 ♘xd4** exd4 9 ♘e2 d5 10 d3 (10 b4 ♗b6 11 ♗b2 d3! 12 ♘g3 ♕d6 13 ♕f3 c6 △ 14 ... h5↑) 10 ... ♗xf5 11 ♘g3 (11

♗f4 ♗d6 {11 ... c6} 12 ♕xd6 ♕xd6 13 ♘xd4 ♘g4 14 g3 ♕h6 15 h4 ♗c8 16 ♕e2 c5!∓ Chandler – Inkiov, Nis 1983) 11 ... ♗g4 12 ♕e1 c6 13 f3 (13 h3 ♖e8 14 ♕d2 ♗d6!? 15 hxg4 ♘xg4 and 16 ... ♕h4) 13 ... ♖e8 14 ♕f2 ♖f8 fxg4?! ♘xg4 16 ♕e2 ♕h4 17 h3 ♕xg3!-+ Planinc – Mariotti, Correspondence 1976/77.

b) **8 ♖e1** ♘g4! 9 ♘e4 ♖xf5! 10 ♘xd4 (10 ♘xc5? ♘xf3+ 11 gxf3 ♘xh2!) 10 ... ♗xd4 11 ♕xg4 d5 and Black has dangerous threats, Vitolinsh – Bojkovic, Rijeka 1963.

c) **8 d3** d5 9 ♘xe5 ♗xf5∓

6 ... ♘xb5

If **6 ... ♗c5** good is 7 ♘xd4! exd4 (7 ... ♗xd4 8 ♘e2 ♗b6 9 d4 e4 {9 ... exd4 10 ♘xd4 0-0 11 ♘e2!} 10 ♘g3 c6 11 ♗e2 0-0 12 f3± Zhilin – Chernov, Rostov 1960) 8 ♖e1+ ♗e7 9 ♘e2 a6 (9 ... 0-0 10 ♘xd4 c5 11 ♘e2!) 10 ♗d3 c5 11 b4! 0-0 12 bxc5 ♗xc5 13 ♘f4!± Matanovic – Janosevic, Sarajevo 1958.

After **6 ... c6** unimpressive is 7 ♗e2 d6 8 ♖e1 (8 ♘xd4 exd4 9 ♗h5+ ♔d7=) allowing 8 ... ♘xf3+! 9 ♗xf3 ♗xf5 and now on 10 d4 follows 10 ... ♕c7! 11 dxe5

(11 ♗f4 0-0-0; 11 ♕e2 0-0-0)
11 ... dxe5 12 ♕e2 (12 ♗f4
♗d6) 12 ... 0-0-0 and Black
is fine. Far stronger (after
6 ... c6) is 7 ♗a4! with the
following possibilities:

a) 7 ... b5 8 ♗b3 ♘xb3 9
axb3 d6 10 d4 e4 11 ♘g5 d5
12 f3±

b) 7 ... d5 8 ♖e1 ♗e7 9
♘xd4 exd4 10 ♘e2 d3 11
♘g3±

c) 7 ... d6 8 ♘xd4 exd4 9
♘e2 ♕a5 10 ♗b3 d3 11 ♘d4
or 11 ♘g3±

d) 7 ... ♗c5 8 ♘xe5 (8
♘xd4 ♗xd4 9 ♘e2± as in
Zhilin - Chernov) 8 ... 0-0 9
♘f3 d5 10 ♘xd4 ♗xd4 11
♘e2± as in Unzicker - Nievergelt in *B2b*. In Govart -
Brem, Reykjavik 1982 9 ...
♘xf5 was tried leading to
10 d4 ♗b4 (10 ... ♗b6 11 d5)
11 ♘e2 d5 12 c3 ♗d6 13 ♗f4
♘e4 14 ♗xd6±

7   ♘xb5   e4

Worth a look are 7 ... c6
8 ♘c3 d5 9 ♘xe5 ♗f5 or 9
♖e1 ♗d6 (9 ... e4) 10 ♘xe5
0-0 with compensation.

8	♖e1	♗e7
9	♘g5	c6
10	♘c3	d5

11   ♘e6

Preferable is 11 d3 but
after 11 ... exd3 12 ♕xd3 0-0
13 ♘e6 ♗xe6 △ 14 ... ♗c5
Black has sufficient counterplay.

11	...	♗xe6
12	fxe6	0-0
13	d3	♗c5!
14	d4	

On 14 ♗e3 d4! follows
and if 14 dxe4 strong is 14
... ♗xf2+ 15 ♔xf2 ♘g4+

14	...	♗d6
15	♗g5	♕e8
16	h3	♕g6
17	♗e3	♖ae8
18	♘e2	♘h5
19	♕d2	♖f3!
20	♔h1	♕xe6

21 ♘g1 ♖g3!

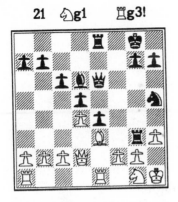

And Black's direct and forceful play has resulted in him obtaining a winning attack, Penson – Gudziev, Yugoslavia 1977.

Black's play in this game is most instructive and will repay careful study. The build up of forces on the kingside and the tactical motifs involving the half-open f-file are particularly worthy of attention.

6) 4 ♘c3 ♘d4

1	e4	e5
2	♘f3	♘c6
3	♗b5	f5
4	♘c3	♘d4

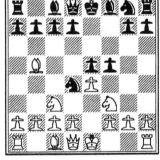

This eccentric looking move was suggested by Alekhine and later analysed in detail by Bulgarian masters.

It looks very curious to move this piece twice in the opening, but by playing 4 ♘c3, White has given up the possibility of c3, and so it is no longer simple to deal with the centralised knight.

White has numerous possible responses, from which we shall discuss the following in detail:

A) 5 exf5
B) 5 ♘e5
C) 5 ♗c4
D) 5 0-0
E) 5 ♗a4

5 ♘xd4 exd4 is too risky, as borne out by the game Karaklajic - Matulovic, Sarajevo 1958, which continued 6 ♘e2 c6 (6 ... fxe4 7 ♘xd4 ♕f6 8 ♘e2 c6 9 ♗a4 d5 is possible) 7 ♗d3 fxe4 8 ♗xe4 d5 9 ♗f3 when after 9 ... d3! there followed 10 cxd3 ♗d6 11 d4 ♘h6 12 0-0 0-0 13 ♘g3 ♕h4 and Black obtained strong attacking chances.

6 exf5 is a tricky move, as Black discovered to his

cost in Kostakiev - Vazov, Bulgaria 1987, e.g. 6 ... dxc3 7 ♕h5+ ♔e7 8 0-0 ♘f6 9 ♖e1+ ♔d6 10 ♕e2! ♔c5 11 a4! c6 12 ♕e3+ ♔b4 13 dxc3+ ♔a5 14 b4+ 1-0. However, 6 ... ♕g5! is a considerable improvement, after which the onus is on White to demonstrate how the attack can be continued.

6 ♘d5!? c6 7 exf5 is interesting. Kostakiev - Kolev, Bulgaria 1986 continued 7 ... cxd5 (7 ... ♕g5! may be preferable, e.g. 8 ♘c7+ ♔d8 9 ♘xa8 ♕xg2 10 ♖f1 cxb5 11 d3 ♘f6 12 c3 ♗c5 13 ♗f4 ♘d5 is good for Black) 8 ♕h5+ ♔e7 9 0-0 ♘f6 10 ♖e1+ ♔d6 11 ♕f3 ♔c7! and White is struggling to find an effective continuation of the attack.

A

5   exf5

5   ...   c6

5 ... ♘xb5 6 ♘xb5 d6 (if 6 ... e4 good is 7 ♘e5 ♘f6 8 ♘g4) 7 d4 e4 8 ♘g5 ♗xf5 9 ♕e2 ♕d7 (9 ... ♘f6 10 ♕c4). The game Parma - Baiaskas, Athens 1980 continued 10 f3 0-0-0 11 fxe4 ♖e8 12 0-0 ♘f6 13 ♖xf5!? ♕xf5 14 ♘xc7 ♖e7 15 ♘b5 ♘xe4 16 ♘xe4 ♖xe4 17 ♕c4+ and now with 17 ... ♕c5! 18 ♕d3 ♕f5 Black could force the repetition of moves. Instead of 10 f3, correct is 10 g4! ♗g6 11 ♘e6±

6   ♘xd4!?

This leads to puzzling complications, reminiscent of Steinitz's Gambit in the Vienna Game.

Alternatively, Wedberg - Brem, Reykjavik 1982 saw 6 ♗e2 ♕f6 (6 ... ♘f6 7 ♘xe5 ♕e7 8 ♘d3 d5 9 0-0 ♗xf5 10 ♘e1 0-0-0 11 d3 ♕c7 12 ♗e3 ♘xe2+ 13 ♘xe2 ♗d6∞ Sax - Romero, Rome 1986) 7 ♘xd4 (7 0-0 d5 8 ♖e1 ♘xf3+ 9 ♗xf3 ♗xf5=) 7 ... exd4 8 ♘e4 ♕xf5 9 ♘g3 ♕f7 10 0-0 d5 11 ♖e1 ♔d8 12 ♗g4 d3! 13 cxd3 ♗c5∞.

After 6 ♗a4 ♕f6! is a good reply 7 0-0 (7 ♘xd4 exd4 8 ♕h5+ ♕f7 9 ♕xf7+ ♔xf7 10 ♘e2 ♗c5 and White cannot hold the extra

pawn) 7 ... d6 8 ♖e1 (if 8
♘d5 ♕f7 or 8 ♘xd4 exd4 9
♕h5+ g6) 8 ... ♘xf3+ 9 ♕xf3
♔d8 is approximately equal.

6 ♘xe5 ♘f6? (6 ... cxb5 7
♕h5+±) 7 ♗d3!± was Nunn –
de la Villa, Szirak 1987, but
Nunn's notes do not men-
tion 6 ... ♕g5! with totally
unexplored complications.

6 ♗d3!? is a radical at-
tempt to defend the f-
pawn. 6 ... ♘xf3+ 7 ♕xf3
♘f6 8 ♕e2 ♕e7 9 b3 d5 10 f3
♗d7 11 ♗b2 0-0-0 12 0-0-0
♖e8 13 ♕f2 ♔b8 14 g4 was
clearly better for White in
Wedberg – de la Villa, Lugano 1988. 6 ... ♘xf3+, developing all of White's
position for him, looks to
be the culprit here. More
to the point is 6 ... ♘f6.

6	...	exd4
7	♕h5+	♔e7
8	0-0	d5!?

A continuation suggested
and analysed by the Italian
master Tatai whose analy-
sis we now follow.

Gheorghiu – Bielicki, Mar
del Plata 1965 saw instead 8
... dxc3 9 dxc3 ♘f6 (9 ... d6?
10 ♗c4 d5 11 ♖e1+ ♔d7 12
♕f7+ ♘e7 13 ♗g5+-) 10 ♖e1+
♔d6 11 ♗f4+ ♔c5 12 ♗e3+
(not 12 b4+? ♔b6) 12 ... ♔d6
13 ♗f4+ eventually drawn.

After 8 ... ♘f6 9 ♖e1+
♔d6 Tatai's analysis gives
10 ♘e4+ (10 ♕h4 ♔c7 11
♕xd4 cxb5 12 ♘xb5+ ♔b8 13
d3 ♕b6 14 ♕xb6 axb6 15
♗f4+ d6 16 ♘xd6 ♗xd6 17
♗xd6+ ♔a7 18 g4±) 10 ...
♘xe4 11 ♖xe4 cxb5 12 d3!
♗e7 13 f6 gxf6 14 ♕xb5 ♔c7
15 ♗f4+ d6 16 ♕c4+ (16 ♕c5+
♔d7 17 ♕b5+ ♔c7 18 ♕c5+
leads only to perpetual
check) 16 ... ♔d7 (16 ... ♔b8
17 ♕f7) 17 ♕e6+ ♔c7 18 ♕f7
♖e8 19 ♖ae1 ♔d7 20 ♖e6!

Let's return to the main
continuation 8 ... d5!?

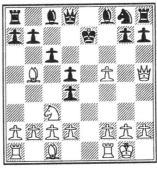

9 ♖e1+

9 b3 is well met by 9 ...
dxc3. Garcia – Tatai, Torre-
molinos 1983 went 10 ♗a3+
♔d7 11 ♕f7+ ♘e7 12 f6 (12
♖fe1 ♕e8! and White's attack comes to a standstill)
12 ... gxf6 13 ♖fe1 ♖g8! 14
♕e6+ (14 ♖e6 ♖g7!) 14 ...
♔c7 15 ♕xf6 ♘g6 16 ♕f7+

♗d7 17 ♕xg8 ♗xa3∓

9	...	♔d6
10	♖e8	

After **10 d3**, the Black king runs away – 10 ... ♘f6 11 ♗f4+ ♔c5! 12 b4+ ♔b6! 13 ♘a4+ (13 a4 a6! 14 ♕f7 ♕d7) 13 ... ♔xb5 14 c4+ dxc3 15 ♘xc3+ ♔a6 16 ♕d1 ♗xb4 and White remains a piece down.

10 ♘xd5!? is another try for White. 10 ... cxd5 11 ♖e8 ♕f6 12 d3 ♘e7 13 ♗g5 ♕xf5 14 ♕h4 ♘c6 15 b4! ♔c7 16 ♗d8+ ♔d7 17 ♖ae1 g5 18 ♕xd4 ♖g8 19 ♖8e5 ♔xd8 20 ♕xd5+ ♔c7 21 ♖xf5 ♗xf5 22 ♕xg8 ♖d8 23 ♗xc6 bxc6 24 ♕xg5 ♗g6 25 ♕a5+ ♔c8 26 h4 ♗d6 27 h5 ♗e8 28 c4 ♗c7 29 ♕f5+ ♔b8 30 ♕xh7 1-0 Seibold – Bruning, Bundesliga 1990.

10	...	♕f6
11	d3	♘e7!
12	♗f4+	

The attack **12 ♗g5 ♕xf5 13 g4!?** is repulsed by 13 ... ♕f3! 14 ♗xe7+ (14 ♖e1 ♗xg4) 14 ... ♗xe7 15 ♖xh8 ♗xg4 16 ♕xh7 ♖xh8 17 ♕xh8 dxc3∓

12	...	♔c5!
13	b4+	♔b6
14	♗g5	

14 a4 a6 (simpler is 14 ... dxc3) 15 a5+ ♔a7 16 ♗a4 dxc3 17 ♗c7 b5! and again

Black keeps the extra piece having beaten off the attack.

| 14 | ... | ♕xf5 |

Here it is difficult to see an effective White continuation, and Black threatens to consolidate the material advantage. The black king has obtained a curious sanctuary on b6.

| 15 | g4 |

15 ♗xe7 ♗xe7 16 ♕xf5 ♗xf5 17 ♖xe7 dxc3 18 ♗a4 and White keeps the material balance but the offside bishop gives Black the chances after 18 ... g6 or 18 ... g5

15	...	♕f3
16	♗xe7	♗xe7
17	♖xh8	♗xg4
18	♕xh7	♖xh8
19	♕xh8	dxc3∓

B)

| 5 | ♘xe5 |

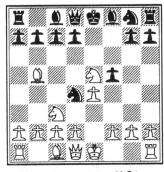

5   ...   ♕f6

This certainly seems to be Black's best. Others lead to a White advantage. For example:

a) 5 ... ♕e7 6 ♕h5+ g6 7 ♘xg6 ♕f7 8 exf5 ♘xc2+ (8 ... hxg6 9 ♕xh8 ♘xc2+ 10 ♔d1 ♘xa1 11 ♖e1+) 9 ♔d1 ♘xa1 10 ♗c4

b) 5 ... ♘f6 6 d3! ♗c5 (if 6 ... fxe4 7 dxe4 ♘xb5 8 ♘xb5 ♕e7, then White has a material plus after 9 ♘xc7+ ♔d8 10 ♘xa8) 7 0-0

c) 5 ... ♕g5 6 0-0 fxe4 7 f4 exf3 8 ♘xf3 ♘xf3+ (8 ... ♕c5 9 ♘xd4 ♕xd4+ 10 ♔h1) 9 ♕xf3 ♗c5+ 10 d4!

6   ♘f3

Mechkarov analysed the continuation 6 f4 fxe4! 7 ♘d5 (7 0-0 is a mistake because of 7 ... ♘xb5 8 ♘xb5 ♕b6+, but Shamkovich's recommendation 7 ♗c4!? deserves attention.

Another move here is 7 ♗a4 which led to interesting play in Miner – Hagglof, Correspondence 1983, e.g. 7 ... ♕h4+! 8 g3 ♕h3 9 ♘xe4 ♕g2 10 ♘f2 ♘f6 11 c3 ♘e4! 12 ♘eg4! ♘f3+ 13 ♔e2 h5↑) 7 ... ♕d6 and came to the conclusion that it is good for Black after 8 ♗c4 (8 ♕h5+ g6 9 ♘xg6 hxg6 10 ♕xh8 ♕xd5 11 c4 ♘c2+ 12 ♔d1 ♕d3!) 8 ... c6 9 ♕h5+ g6 10 ♘xg6 hxg6 11 ♕xh8 ♘xc2+ 12 ♔d1 ♘xa1.

6   ...   ♘xb5

6 ... fxe4 7 ♘xd4 (7 ♘xe4 ♘xf3+ 8 ♕xf3 ♕xf3 9 gxf3 c6 10 ♗e2 d5 11 ♘g3 ♗h3 is better for Black despite the pawn deficit) 7 ... ♕xd4 8 0-0 c6 9 ♗a4 ♘f6 (9 ... d5 10 d3 exd3 11 ♗e3 ♕g4 12 ♕xd3±) 10 d3 exd3 11 ♖e1+ ♔f7 12 ♗e3 ♕h4 13 ♕xd3 d5 14 ♗d4 ♗d6 15 g3 Frid – Schmidt, Correspondence 1958. Now, instead of 15 ... ♕g5? 16 ♗xf6 ♕xf6 17 ♘xd5!+– Black should have played 15 ... ♕h5 with equal chances.

7   ♘xb5   fxe4
8   ♕e2   ♕e7
9   ♘fd4

9 ♘xc7+? ♔d8 10 ♘xa8 exf3∓

9   ...   d6

10	0-0	♘f6
11	d3	a6
12	♘c3	♗g4

Here Black has equal play thanks to the potential activity of the bishop pair.

13   f3!

13 ♕e3 exd3 14 ♕xd3 0-0-0 15 ♗g5 ♕d7 16 ♖fe1 c5 with the initiative, Zaharian - Nikitin, Moscow 1963.

13	...	exf3
14	♕f2!	

14 ♕xe7+ ♗xe7 simplifies Black's task of utilising the bishops.

14	...	0-0-0
15	♘xf3	♔b8
16	♗g5	h6
17	♖ae1	♕f7=

Black can hold his own here, Bobolovich - Nikitin, Moscow 1963.

C

5	♗c4

5	...	c6

The best response. If 5 ... d6 then 6 exf5! gives White excellent chances. For example 6 ... ♘f6 (6 ... ♗xf5 7 ♘xd4 exd4 8 ♕f3! ♗g6 9 ♕xb7 dxc3 10 ♕c6+ ♔e7 11 0-0 ♕c8 12 ♖e1+ ♔d8 13 ♗e6 ♘e7 14 ♕f3 ♕b8 15 dxc3 with a decisive attack for the sacrificed piece, Kirianov - Remeniuk, Semi-Final Ukraine Ch. 1959) 7 0-0! ♗xf5 (7 ... ♘xf5 8 ♖e1 △ (d4) 8 ♘xd4 exd4 9 ♖e1+ ♗e7 10 ♘e2 c5 11 ♘f4 d5 12 ♘xd5! ♘xd5 13 ♕f3± (Euwe)

6 d3 (instead of 6 exf5!) 6 ... ♘f6 can lead to interesting play, e.g. 7 ♘xd4 (7 ♗g5 h6 8 ♘xe5 hxg5 9 ♘f7 ♕b6 10 ♘xh8 ♕xb2 11 0-0 ♕xc3 12 e5 ♕xc2 13 exf6 ♕xd1 14 ♗f7+ ♔d8 15 ♖axd1 gxf6 16 ♖de1 ♗c5 17 ♔h1 b5 18 f4 ♔c7 19 ♖e8 a5 20 ♗g6 b4 21 fxg5 fxg5 22 ♘f7 a4

23 ♘xg5 b3 and Black went on to win in Antunes – de la Villa Garcia, Andorra Zonal 1987) 7 ... exd4 8 ♘e2 fxe4 9 dxe4 ♘xe4 10 ♕xd4 ♘f6 11 ♗g5 c6 12 0-0-0 d5 13 ♘f4 ♗e7 14 ♘xd5! cxd5 15 ♗xf6 gxf6 16 ♗xd5 ♗f5 17 ♕f4 ♕c8 18 ♗b3 ♗e6 19 ♗xe6 ♕xe6 20 ♖de1 ♕xa2 21 ♕c7 0-0 22 ♖xe7 ♕a1+ 23 ♔d2 ♖ad8+ 24 ♔e3 1-0 Abramovic – Kovacevic, Novi Sad 1985.

However, Black does better to take the chance for 6 ... ♗e7! (6 ... ♘xf3+ 7 ♕xf3 ♘f6 8 ♗g5 {8 exf5 c6 then ... d5} 8 ... c6 9 0-0-0 h6! 10 ♗xf6 ♕xf6= Halifman – Inkiov, Plovdiv 1982) 7 ♘xd4 exd4 8 ♘e2 ♗f6 9 0-0 c6 10 ♘g3 ♗e7 Faibisovich – Korolev, Leningrad 1962).

6   0-0

Alternatives:

a) **6 ♗xg8** ♖xg8 7 0-0 d6 (7 ... ♕f6 8 exf5 d5! 9 ♘xe5 ♘xc2∞) 8 ♖e1 ♘xf3+ 9 ♕xf3 f4 10 d4 (10 ♕h5+ g6 11 ♕xh7 ♖g7∞) 10 ... g5 11 dxe5 dxe5 12 ♘e2 (mistaken are 12 ♕h5+ ♖g6 13 ♕xh7? ♖h6 14 ♕g8 ♗e6 and 12 ♖d1 ♕c7 13 ♕d3 ♗e6) 12 ... ♗e6 13 ♕c3 ♗d6 14 b3 ♕b6 15 ♗b2 0-0-0∓

b) After **6 d3** ♘xf3+ 7 ♕xf3 ♕f6 8 ♕e2 (8 exf5 ♘e7!; 8 0-0 fxe4 9 ♕xe4 ♗e7 or 8 ♗xg8 ♖xg8 9 exf5 d5 all leave Black the better chances) 8 ... f4! Black has good play. For example 9 ♗d2 ♘e7 10 0-0-0 d6 11 f3 ♗d7 12 ♕f2 g5 13 h4 g4 and Black's position is preferable, Westerinen – Lanka, Jurmala 1978.

c) **6 ♘xe5**

Now 6 ... ♕f6 is risky as after 7 ♘f3! fxe4 8 ♘xd4 ♕xd4 9 d3 d5 10 ♗e3 ♕f6 11 ♗xd5! cxd5 12 ♘xd5 White obtains a very strong attack for the piece. The right continuation is 6 ... ♕e7! when after 7 ♕h5+ (7 ♘f7 d5 8 ♘xh8 dxc4 9 0-0 ♗e6 △ ... 0-0-0) 7 ... g6 8 ♘xg6 ♘f6 9 ♘xe7+ (9 ♕h4 hxg6 10 ♕xh8 fxe4) 9 ... ♘xh5 10 ♘xc8 ♘xc2+ 11 ♔d1 ♘xa1 12 exf5 d5 13 ♗e2 ♘f4

Black stands well.

6 ... d6

In Bogolyubov - Reti, Stockholm 1919, Black played poorly - 6 ... ♘xf3+? 7 ♕xf3 ♕f6 8 d4! exd4 9 e5! ♕h4 10 ♘e2 ♗c5 11 b4!±

A better alternative is **6 ... ♘f6!?** If White now tries 7 ♖e1 then with 7 ... ♘xf3+ 8 ♕xf3 fxe4! 9 ♘xe4 d5 10 ♘xf6+ ♕xf6 11 ♕h5+ ♔d8 Black gets good play. Better is 7 ♘xe5 fxe4 (7 ... ♕e7? 8 exf5) 8 ♘f7 ♕c7! (8 ... ♕e7 9 ♘xh8 d5 10 ♗e2 ♗f5 11 d3 0-0-0 12 ♗e3 ♘xe2+ 13 ♘xe2± Geller - Rodriguez, Las Palmas 1976) 9 ♘xh8 d5 10 ♗xd5 cxd5 11 ♘xd5 ♕e5! 12 ♘xf6+ gxf6∓, and if instead 10 ♗e2 ♗d6 (10 ... ♗f5) 11 ♗h5+ g6 12 ♘xg6 ♗xh2+ 13 ♔h1 hxg6 14 ♗xg6+ ♔e7 Black has a good attacking position for the exchange.

7 ♖e1

Others:

a) 7 ♘xd4 exd4 8 ♘e2 fxe4 9 ♘xd4 ♕f6∓

b) 7 d3 ♘xf3+ 8 ♕xf3 and now after 8 ... f4! 9 g3 ♕g5 or 9 h3 ♕h4 Black gets good play. Mechkarov's recommendation 8 ... ♕f6 is well met by 9 exf5 d5 10 ♗b3 ♗xf5 11 ♕g3 ♗d6 12 ♗g5 ♕g6 13 ♖ae1 and White has chances for the initiative, Zacharov - Nikitin, Moscow 1962.

c) 7 exf5 ♗xf5 (7 ... d5 8 ♘xe5 ♘f6 9 ♖e1 ♗e7 10 ♗d3 ♘xf5 or 10 ... 0-0 with compensation; 7 ... ♘xf5 8 ♖e1 ♗e7 9 ♗b3 ♘f6 10 d3 {10 ♘g5 d5 11 ♖xe5 0-0} 10 ... ♕b6 11 h3 ♖f8! 12 g4 ♘xg4! 13 hxg4 ♘h4 with a strong attack, Novopashin - Babenishev, Ukraine 1962) 8 ♘xd4 (8 d3 ♘f6) 8 ... exd4 9 ♖e1+ ♔d7 with sharp play.

7 ... ♘xf3+
8 ♕xf3 f4
9 d4

9 ♗xg8 ♖xg8∓ 9 g3 ♕f6 10 d4 (better 10 gxf4 ♕xf4 11 ♕xf4 exf4 12 d4 g5=) 10 ... g5 11 dxe5 (11 ♗d2 h5 12 gxf4 gxf4 13 h3 ♕h4 14 ♔h2 ♘f6 15 ♘e2 ♗h6! 16 ♗c3 ♗xh3-+ Kryukov - Popov, Correspondence 1961/62) 11

... dxe5 12 ♕h5+ ♕g6 13 ♕xg6+ hxg6 14 ♗d2 ♘f6 15 h4 ♘g4 16 ♔g2 ♗c5 17 ♖f1 gxh4∓ Yoffie - Yudasin, Leningrad 1978.

9	...	♕f6
10	b4!	♘e7
11	d5	h5

12	dxc6	bxc6
13	b5	♗e6
14	♗xe6	

14 ♗d3!?

14	...	♕xe6
15	♖d1	♘g6
16	bxc6	♘h4
17	♕e2	

17 ♕d3 ♕g4 18 g3 ♘f3+ 19 ♔g2 h4 20 h3 hxg3 and, if anybody, it is Black who is for preference.

17	...	♖c8
18	c7?!	♖xc7
19	♘d5	♖c8
20	♖b1	♔f7
	½ : ½	

Goldstein - Rozumenko, Correspondence 1983.

D

5	0-0	c6
6	♗a4	

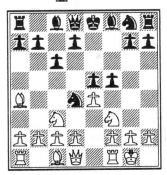

6	...	d6

Black's alternatives:

a) 6 ... ♘f6 7 exf5± see Chapter 5, B3.

b) 6 ... ♕f6 7 d3 ♘xf3+ 8 ♕xf3 f4 9 d4 d6 10 dxe5 dxe5 11 ♘d5 ♕d6 12 ♖d1 ♘f6 13 ♘xf4 ♗g4 14 ♖xd6 ♗xf3 15 ♖xc6± Rivera - Santos, Lucerne 1982.

c) 6 ... b5 7 ♗b3 ♘xb3 8 axb3 b4 9 ♘e2 fxe4 10 ♘xe5 ♘f6 11 ♘g3! ♕c7 12 ♘g4 ♘xg4 13 ♕xg4 d5 14 ♕g5 ♕e7 (14 ... ♗d6 15 d3! 0-0 16 dxe4± Black has no compensation for his numerous weaknesses) 15 ♕e3 ♕c5 16 d4 ♕e7 17 f3 exf3 18 ♕xf3± Nemet - Bojkovic, Skopje 1962. White has a useful lead in development.

d) 6 ... ♕a5 7 exf5! d6 8 ♖b1! b5 (8 ... ♗d7 9 ♘xd4

exd4 10 b4 ♕a6 {10 ... ♕b6 11
♕h5+ ♔d8 12 ♘e2} 11 ♕h5+
♔d8 12 b5 ♕a5 13 ♕h4+!+−) 9
♘xd4! exd4 10 ♗b3 ♘f6 (10
... dxc3 11 ♕h5+ ♔d8 12
♗xg8 cxd2 13 ♕g5+ ♗e7 14
♕xg7 dxc1♕ 15 ♖bxc1+−) 11
♕e2+ ♔d8 12 ♘e4± Anders-
son – Schmidt, Correspondence 1959.

7 ♖e1

7 exf5 is a serious alternative when Black can consider:

a) **7 ... ♕a5 8 ♖b1!** as in
Andersson – Schmidt above.

b) **7 ... ♕f6 8 ♖e1 ♔d8 9
d3 ♘xf3+ 10 ♕xf3 ♕xf5=**

c) **7 ... ♗xf5 8 ♘xd4 exd4
9 ♖e1+** (9 ♕f3 ♕d7 10 ♖e1+
♘e7 11 ♘e2 ♕e6±) **9 ... ♔d7
10 ♕f3 g6 11 ♘e2** and now,
not 11 ... ♕f6 when 12 b4!
(Tukmakov – Bojkovic, Vrnjacka Banja 1965) is good
for White, but 11 ... ♗g7!=

7 ... ♕a5

**7 ... ♘f6 8 ♘xd4 exd4 9
♘d5 fxe4 10 d3 e3** (10 ...
♘xd5 11 ♕h5+)∞ Rubenchik
– Goldenov, Vitebsk 1960.

8 exf5

**8 ♖b1 b5 9 ♘xd4 exd4 10
♗b3** doesn't succeed on
account of 10 ... dxc3 11
♕h5+ ♔d8 12 ♗xg8 g6!

8 ... ♔d8!

Mistaken is **8 ... ♗e7?** as

after 9 ♘xd4 exd4 10 ♘e4!
♕xa4 11 ♘xd6+ ♔f8 12 ♕h5
White wins.

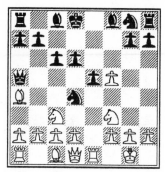

This position promises a
sharp, uncompromising st-
ruggle.

9 a3

White can try to play
more actively, viz **9 b4!?**
♕xb4 10 ♖b1 ♕a5 11 ♗a3 but
Black can then organise
counterplay with 11 ... ♘f6
12 ♘g5 ♔c7 13 ♗b4 ♕a6 14
f4 b5. Gurgenidze – Boyar-
inov, Minsk 1964 continued
15 ♘f7 bxa4! 16 ♘xh8 ♗xf5
17 d3 c5 18 ♗a3 exf4 19 ♕d2
f3 20 ♘f7 h6 21 ♕f4 ♕c6 22
♗b2 ♖b8 23 ♘e4 ♘e2+ 24
♖xe2 fxe2 25 ♕xf5 ♖xb2 26
♖e1 ♕d7−+

9	...	♗xf5
10	b4	♕b6
11	d3	♗g4
12	♗e3	♘f6!
13	♗xd4	exd4
14	♘e4	♘d5

With equal chances, Nilsson - Olsson, Stockholm 1964.

E

5   ♗a4

This bishop retreat was for a long time considered the strongest continuation, and gave Black many unpleasant experiences. But ways have been found for Black to obtain full counterplay.

5   ...   ♘f6

The most promising line. After 5 ... **c6**, White has a strong reply in 6 ♘xe5! If 6 ... ♘f6 then 7 0-0 fxe4 8 ♘xe4 ♘xe4 9 ♖e1! d5 10 d3! gives White the advantage.

Mechkarov suggests 6 ... ♕f6 as an alternative to 6 ... ♘f6, but Black still has difficulties following 7 f4. For example:

a) **7 ... b5** 8 ♗b3 ♘xb3 9 axb3 b4 10 ♘e2 fxe4 11 ♘g3! d5 12 d4 exd3 13 ♕xd3 ±

b) **7 ♘d3** fxe4 (7 ... ♗d6 8 0-0 ♘e7 9 ♖e1) 8 ♘xe4 ♕g6 9 ♘g3 d5 10 ♘f4 ♕f7 11 c3 ♘e6 12 ♘xe6 ♗xe6 13 d4 and Black has no compensation for the pawn.

6   0-0

6 ♘xe5 fxe4 7 0-0 and now 7 ... ♗c5 is a mistake in view of 8 ♘g4! 0-0 9 ♘xf6+ ♕xf6 10 ♘xe4 ♕h4 11 ♘xc5 ♘f3+ 12 gxf3 ♖f5 13 ♕e2±. Correct is 7 ... ♗d6! 8 ♘c4 ♗e7 9 ♘xe4 (9 d3 exd3 10 ♕xd3 ♘e6) 9 ... ♘xe4 10 ♕g4 0-0 11 ♕xe4 ♘f3+! 12 gxf3 d5=

7 ♘g4 (instead of 7 0-0) is possible. A possible continuation is 7 ... ♗e7 8 0-0 0-0 9 ♘xf6+ ♗xf6 10 ♘xe4 d5 11 ♘xf6+ ♕xf6 12 c3 b5! 13 ♗b3 ♘xb3 14 ♕xb3 c6 15 d4 ♕g6∞

6   ...   ♗c5

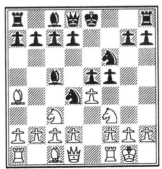

6 ... fxe4 is not so good after 7 ♘xd4 exd4 8 ♘xe4! ♘xe4 9 ♕h5+

6 ... c6 7 exf5! transposes to a good line for White from the fifth chapter (variation B3).

7   ♘xe5

7 ♘xd4 exd4 8 ♘d5 0-0 9 d3 fxe4 10 ♗g5 c6 (10 ... ♗e7) 11 ♘xf6+ gxf6 12 ♗h6 ♖f7 13 ♕g4+ ♔h8 14 ♕h5 ♕e7 15 dxe4 d6 16 ♗b3 ♗e6 17 ♖ad1 ♗xb3 18 axb3 d5∞ Kochiev–Gutman, Baku 1977.

7   ...   0-0

7 ... b5? 8 ♘xb5 fxe4 9 c3 ♘xb5 10 ♗xb5 0-0 11 d4± Balanel - Korchnoi, Ploesti 1957.

7 ... fxe4 8 d3 or 8 ♘g4 are both good.

7 ... c6 8 b4!? ♗b6 9 ♘c4 ♗c7 10 e5± Kupreichik - Bellon, Barcelona 1984.

8   ♘d3

8 exf5 d5! is excellent for Black (again as in Chapter five, B3).

8   ...   fxe4!

An unexpected blow! This surprising and deep piece sacrifice generates excellent play for Black.

8 ... ♗b6 9 e5 ♘e4 10 ♘d5± is feeble in comparison.

9   ♘xc5   d5

10 d3

At first sight, Black piece sacrifice appears to be highly optimistic, but analysis serves to demonstrate that it is by no means easy for White to defend himself.

Alternatives;

a) **10 h3** ♕d6 11 ♘b3 ♘f3+! 12 gxf3 ♗xh3-+

b) **10 f3** exf3 11 gxf3 ♗h3 12 ♖f2 ♘g4! 13 fxg4 ♕h4!-+

c) **10 ♘b5** ♗g4 11 ♕e1 ♘f3+ (11 ... ♘e2+ 12 ♔h1 ♘f4 is also good) 12 gxf3 ♗xf3 with the decisive threats of 13 ... ♕c8 or 13 ... ♘g4.

d) **10 ♘b3** ♗g4 11 f3 (11 ♘xd4 ♗xd1 12 ♘xd1 ♕d6! and Black won, Georgiev - Inkiov, Bulgaria 1980/81) 11 ... exf3 12 gxf3 ♘xf3+ 13 ♖xf3 ♗xf3! 14 ♕xf3 ♘e4 15 ♕g4 ♕f6 16 ♕g2 ♕h4 0 : 1 Tsveifel - Glazkov, Gelendzik 1977.

e) **10 ♗b3 ♔h8 11 ♗xd5**
(only thus can White alleviate the immediate danger)
11 ... ♘xd5 12 ♘5xe4 (12
♘3xe4 ♘f4 13 d3 ♘xg2! 14
♔xg2 ♕h4 15 f4 ♗g4 16 ♕e1
♗f3+ 17 ♔g1 ♘e2+) 12 ...
♘b4! 13 d3 ♘bxc2 14 ♗g5
♕d7 15 ♖c1 ♘b4. Lehmann –
Spassky, Vienna 1957 con-
tinued 16 ♕a4? (Taimanov
and Furman recommend 16
a3, ♗e3 anf f3) 16 ... ♕xa4 17
♘xa4 ♘e2+ 18 ♔h1 ♘xc1 and
Black won.

10 ...   ♘g4
Lehmann recommends
continuing the attack with
10 ... ♗g4 11 ♕d2 b6.

11 ♘5xe4
White must return the
piece, as 11 dxe4? ♕h4 12 h3
♘xf2 and 11 h3? ♕h4 12
hxg4 ♘f3+ are catastrophic.

11 ...   dxe4
12 ♘xe4   ♕h4
13 h3

13 ...   ♘e5!
The reckless piece sac-
rifice 13 ... ♘f3+? 14 gxf3
leaves Black unable to jus-
tify his investment:

a) **14 ... ♕xh3** 15 fxg4
♗xg4 16 ♘g5! ♕h4 17 ♕e1!
♗f3 18 ♕e6+

b) **14 ... ♘h2** 15 ♔xh2
♕xh3+ 16 ♔g1 ♖xf3 17 ♗b3+
♔h8 18 ♕d2

c) **14 ... ♘e5** 15 f4 ♕xh3 16
f3

In all cases White has a
winning advantage (Taim-
anov and Furman)

14 f4
Vukcevic – Matulovic,
Sarajevo saw the weaker **14
♗b3+ ♔h8 15 ♘g5?** (15 f4
♗g4 16 ♕d2 ♘e2+! 17 ♔h2
♖ae8! △ 18 ... ♘f3+ with ...
♖xe4 following and White
has no satisfactory de-
fence) 15 ... ♘ef3+ 16 gxf3
♗xh3 and Black won.

14 ...   ♗g4

15 ♕d2

Of course not **15 ♕e1?** ♘ef3+!

15 ...   ♗f3!!

An excellent resource, discovered by Mechkarov. After **15 ... ♘e2+ 16 ♔h2** Black's attack is stillborn.

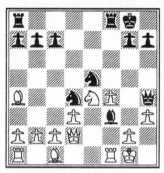

16 ♘c3

Mechkarov claims this is White's best chance. The alternative is **16 fxe5 ♗xe4!** 17 dxe4 ♖xf1+ 18 ♔xf1 ♖f8+ 19 ♔g1 ♘f3+ 20 gxf3 ♖xf3 resulting in a highly unclear position. White is best advised to take the safer course of the text continuation.

16 ...   ♖f6
17 ♕f2   ♖g6
18 ♕xh4   ♖xg2+
19 ♔h1   ♖f2+=

A very instructive variation which emphatically demonstrates the value of the initiative.

7) 4 ♞c3 fxe4 5 ♞xe4
without 5 ... d5

1	e4	e5
2	♞f3	♞c6
3	♗b5	f5
4	♞c3	fxe4
5	♞xe4	

Currently the most popular continuation. Here we concern ourselves with the Black tries

A) 5 ... ♗e7
B) 5 ... ♞f6

5 ... **d5** is considered in the eighth and ninth chapters.

5 ... **a6** is weak. Gurgenidze - Lein, Baku 1961 continued 6 ♗xc6 bxc6 7 d4 d5 8 ♞xe5 (8 ♞g3) 8 ... dxe4 9 ♕h5+ g6 10 ♞xg6 ♞f6 11 ♕e5+ ♔f7 12 ♞xh8+ ♔g8 13 ♗g5 ♗g7 14 ♗xf6 ♕xf6 15 ♕e8+ ♕f8 16 ♕xc6±

A)

5   ...   ♗e7

This should not be good for Black but White is forced to counter energetically.

6   **d4!**

Best. Other continuations pose less problems:

a) **6 ♗xc6** dxc6 7 ♕e2 ♗g4 8 h3 ♗xf3 9 ♕xf3 ♘f6 10 ♘xf6+ ♗xf6 11 ♕b3! ♕d5! 12 ♕xb7 ♕xg2 13 ♕xa8+ (13 ♖f1 ♔d7) 13 ... ♔d7 14 ♕xh8 ♕e4+ 15 ♔f1 ♕xh1+ 16 ♔e2 ♕e4+ ½ : ½ Keller - Duckstein, Bad Pyrmont 1963.

b) **6 0-0** d5! 7 ♘g3 ♗g4 8 h3 ♗xf3 9 ♕xf3 ♘f6 10 ♕c3 (if 10 ♕e2, Kapengut recommends 10 ... 0-0 11 ♗xc6 bxc6 12 ♕xe5 ♗d6⩲; 10 ♕f5 is met by 10 ... ♕d7). White wins a pawn, but Black gains sufficient counterchances with 10 ... ♕d7 (10 ... 0-0 11 ♗xc6 bxc6 12 ♕xc6 ♗d6! {12 ... ♕c8? 13 c4± Kapengut - Marjasin, 1976} 13 c4 e4 14 cxd5 ♗xg3 15 fxg3 ♕xd5⩲) 11 ♗xc6 bxc6 12 ♕xe5 0-0 13 ♕f5 ♗c5 14 ♕xd7 ♘xd7 15 d3 ♖ae8 16 ♗d2 h5 17 ♖ae1 ♖xe1 18 ♗xe1 h4 19 ♘e2 ♖e8⩲ Nezhmetdinov - Lein, Vologda 1962. Black succeeded in holding the balance.

c) **6 ♕e2** ♘d4! (6 ... ♘f6 7 ♘g3! - see below) 7 ♘xd4 exd4 8 ♕h5+ ♔f8 9 ♗c4 ♕e8 10 ♕xe8+ ♔xe8 11 0-0 c6 12 ♗e2 d5 13 ♘g3 (Teschner - Duckstein, Salzburg 1961) 13 ... g6! with good play.

d) **6 ♘g3** ♘f6?! (correct is 6 ... ♘d4! as in the preceding example) 7 ♕e2 0-0 8 ♗xc6 dxc6 9 0-0 ♗d6 10 ♘xe5 ♖e8 11 d4 c5 12 ♗g5 cxd4 13 f4± Kuporosov - Jandemirov, Kostroma 1985.

6   ...   exd4

6 ... d5 7 ♘eg5! h6 8 ♘h3!⩲

7   0-0

7 ♘xd4 ♘f6 8 ♘xf6+ (8 ♘g3 0-0 9 ♘df5 d5 10 0-0? {10 ♘xe7+ ♕xe7+ 11 ♕e2= had to be played} 10 ... ♗c5 11 c3 ♗xf5 12 ♘xf5 ♘e4 13 ♘e3 ♘e5 14 ♗e2 c6 with a tremendous position for Black, Kayumov - Nadezhdin, Uzbekistan 1971) 8 ... ♗xf6 9 ♘xc6 bxc6 10 ♕e2+ ♗e7= Ivkov - Duckstein, Zagreb 1955.

7   ...   d5

7 ... ♘f6 proves unsatisfactory after 8 ♘xf6+ ♗xf6 9 ♖e1+ ♘e7 (9 ... ♔f8 10 ♗f4 d6 {Holaczek - Duckstein, Vienna 1973} is doubtful, e.g. 11 ♗xc6 bxc6 12 ♘xd4 c5 13 ♘e6+ ♗xe6 14 ♖xe6 ♖b8 15 ♕f3 and Black is under great pressure and will find it difficult to repulse the attack) 10 ♘g5 0-0 11 ♘xh7! with a decisive attack as in the game Trifunovic - Kostic, Rogatska Zlatina 1939.

8 ♘eg5!

Only this continuation, in conjunction with the sacrifice of a piece, gives White chances for the advantage.

Instead, **8 ♘g3 ♗g4 9 h3 ♗xf3 10 ♕xf3** is not so dangerous for Black, as the game Voitsek - Nadezhdin, Correspondence 1978, demonstrates - 10 ... ♘f6! 11 ♘f5 0-0 12 ♗xc6 bxc6 13 ♘xd4 ♘e4 14 ♕g4 ♕d6 15 ♗e3 (15 ♘f5 ♕f6 16 ♗h6 ♖f7 and White's attack is petering out) 15 ... g6 16 ♖ad1 ♖f6 17 c4 h5=

8	**...**	**h6**

8 ... ♕d6 9 ♕xd4 ♗f6 10 ♕a4 ♘ge7 11 ♗f4±

9	**♗xc6+**	**bxc6**
10	**♘f7!**	**♔xf7**
11	**♘e5+**	**♔f6**
12	**♕xd4!**	

After **12 ♕h5? ♗f5 13 ♕f7+ ♔xe5** Black can avoid being mated while maintaining the material plus, e.g. 14 ♘f4+ (14 ♖e1+ ♔d6 15 ♕xf5 ♔c5) 14 ... ♔xf4 15 ♖ae1 g6 16 g3+ (Zaitsev - Lisenko, 1964) and now with 16 ... ♔g5! Black could have achieved a decisive advantage.

12	**...**	**c5**
13	**♕f4+**	**♗f5**
14	**h4!**	

14 g4 ♕c8 15 ♖e1 g5! 16 ♕f3 ♘d6! 17 ♕xd5 ♗e6 18 ♕e4 ♘e7 19 b4 ♗d5 20 ♕e3 ♕e6 21 ♗b2 ♗xe5! 22 ♗xe5+ ♔f7∓ Han - Nadezhdin, Tashkent 1971.

14 ♘g4+ ♔g6 15 ♘e5+ ♔f6 16 g4 ♕c8 17 ♖e1 g5!∓

White's attack is very strong as is demonstrated by practice.

14	**...**	**♗d6**

Better than the text, but also insufficient for equality is **14 ... g6**. The correspondence game Voloshin - Nadezhdin 1978 showed the way for White 15 b4! ♔g7 16 ♗b2 ♘f6 17 g4 ♗e6 (Black has kept the extra piece but the White attack continues) 18 ♖fe1 d4 19 ♘c6 ♕d7 20 ♘xe7 ♕xe7 21 bxc5 g5 22 ♕xd4! and White's advantage is not in doubt.

15	♖e1	♘e7
16	g4	♗xe5
17	♕xe5+	♔f7
18	gxf5	♕d6
19	♕e6+	♕xe6
20	fxe6+	♔g6
21	♗f4	♖ac8
22	♖ad1	♖he8
23	c4!±	

Black lost on time! Voloshin - Savchenko, 1970.

B

5   ...   ♘f6

This simple developing move was not seen in serious tournaments for many decades, because it was assumed that after 6 ♘xf6+ ♕xf6 7 ♕e2 Black was losing a pawn without compensation. However, times have changed and statistics show that many modern exponents of the Jaenisch give preference to 5 ... ♘f6.

Now there are two White moves worthy of consideration:

B1) 6 ♘xf6+
B2) 6 ♕e2

6 ♗xc6 dxc6 7 ♕e2 was examined in the first chapter.

B1

6   ♘xf6+

6   ...   ♕xf6!

Only thus. 6 ... **gxf6** proves unsatisfactory after 7 d4. Bardeleben - Leonhardt, Vienna 1908 saw 7 ... d6 (7 ... e4 8 ♘g5! ♗b4+ 9 c3 fxg5 10 ♕h5+ ♔f8 11 ♗xg5 ♘e7 12 ♗c4 d5 13 ♗xd5! 1 : 0 Brinckmann - Kieninger, Ludwigshafen 1932) 8 d5! a6 9 ♗e2 ♘e7 10 ♘h4 c6 (10 ... ♘g6 11 ♗h5 ♖g8 12 ♕d3 ♔f7 13 f4 exf4 14 0-0±) 11 ♗h5+ ♔d7 12 dxc6+ bxc6 13 c4!

with a long term initiative.

We now have the further dichotomy:

B11) 7 0-0
B12) 7 ♕e2

Others do not test Black, e.g. 7 ♗xc6 dxc6 8 ♕e2 ♗g4! 9 ♕xe5+ ♗e7 reaching a favourable position from the main line, or 7 **d4** ♘xd4! 8 ♘xd4 exd4 9 0-0 ♗e7 10 ♕h5+ g6 11 ♕h6 c6 12 ♖e1 ♔f7! 13 ♖xe7+? (13 ♗c4+) 13 ... ♕xe7 14 ♗g5 ♕e5-+ Neuronov - Ivanov, Tbilisi 1973.

B11

7 0-0

7 ... ♘d4

7 ... ♗e7 gives White various options:

a) **8 ♕e2** ♘d4 leads to the main line.

b) **8 ♖e1** 0-0 (8 ... ♘d4 is the main line) 9 ♗xc6 dxc6

10 d4 (10 d3 ♗d6) 10 ... ♗g4= (Belavenets).

c) **8 ♗xc6** dxc6 (worse is 8 ... bxc6 9 ♕e1! d6 10 d4±) 9 ♕e1 0-0 (9 ... e4 10 ♕xe4 ♗f5) 10 d3 ♗d6 11 ♘g5 ♕g6 12 ♘e4 ♗h3 13 ♘g3 ♗g4=

8 ♘xd4 exd4
9 ♖e1+

Others:

a) **9 ♕h5+** g6 10 ♖e1+ ♗e7 leads to the main variation.

b) **9 ♗e2** ♗e7 10 d3 0-0 11 ♗f3 c6 12 ♗d2 d5= Liang - Hjorth, Thessaloniki 1984.

c) **9 d3** ♗e7 10 ♕h5+ g6 11 ♕h6 c6 12 ♗a4 d5 13 ♗d2 ♔f7 14 ♖ae1 ♗f8 15 ♕f4 ♕xf4 16 ♗xf4 ♗g7= Kruppa - Jandemirov, 1985.

d) **9 b3** ♗e7 (9 ... c6 10 ♗c4 (Tal recommends 10 ♗d3 d5 11 c4 {11 ♕e2+ ♗e6! 12 ♗b2 ♔f7!} 11 ... ♗e6! 12 cxd5 ♗xd5 13 ♕g4 (13 ♕e2+ ♕e6) 13 ... h5∞) 10 ... b5! 11 ♖e1+ ♗e7 12 ♗d3 0-0 13 ♕e2 d5 14 ♕xe7 ♕xf2+ 15 ♔h1 ♗h3 16 ♖g1 ♖ae8∞ Friedrich - Schlesinger, Hungary 1988). 10 ♗b2 c6 11 ♗d3 d5 12 ♕e2 ♔f7!? 13 ♖ae1 ♗d6 14 f4 ♗d7 15 ♕f2 c5 16 ♕f3 ♗c6 17 f5 ♗e5 (17 ... ♖he8) 18 ♕h5+ ♔e7 19 ♖f2 ♔d7 Thiemann - Kitev, Correspondence 1982.

9 ... ♗e7
10 ♕e2

The manoeuvre **10 ♕h5+ g6 11 ♕h6** is not dangerous for Black after 11 ... c6 12 d3 ♔f7 13 ♗a4! (13 ♖xe7+? ♕xe7 14 ♗g5 ♕e5 and Black won in Platonov – Ivanov, Riga 1975) 13 ... d5 14 ♗f4 ♗f8 15 ♕g5 ♕xg5 16 ♗xg5 ♗f5=

10   ...   c6

10 ... b6 11 f3 ♗b7 12 b3±

11   ♗d3

11 ♗a4 came unstuck in Leminski – Ehrke, Bundesliga 1987. Black developed a strong initiative and after 11 ... d5 12 ♕h5+ ♕f7 13 ♕e5 0-0 14 f3 ♗h4 15 ♖f1 ♗f6 16 ♕d6 ♗f5 17 d3 ♖ae8 18 ♗f4 ♖e6 19 ♕b4 ♗d8 20 ♗b3 ♗xd3 21 cxd3 ♕xf4 22 ♕xb7 ♖h6 23 g3 ♕e3+ 24 ♔g2 ♕e2+ 25 ♖f2 ♖xh2+ he went on to win.

11   ...   d5

11 ... d6!? 12 b3 0-0! 13 ♕xe7 ♕xf2+ 14 ♔h1 ♗h3 15 ♕e4!? ♗xg2+ 16 ♕xg2 ♕xe1+ 17 ♕g1 ♕f2!? 18 ♕xf2 ♖xf2 19 ♗b2 c5 20 ♔g1! ♖af8 21 ♖e1 ♖xd2 22 ♗c1 ♖df2 23 ♖e7= Shatskes – Auzinch, 1984.

12   b3

12 c3 ♗d7 13 cxd4 (13 f3 ♔f7!) 13 ... 0-0!

12 f3 ♔f7 13 b3 ♗d6 14 ♗b2 ♗e6∓ Zauerman – Ivan-ov, Correspondence 1979.

12   ...   0-0

12 ... ♔f7 is bad, e.g 13 ♗b2 ♗d6 14 c4±

13   ♕xe7   ♕xf2+
14   ♔h1   ♗h3
15   ♖g1!?

Here, White can, if he wishes, make a draw by **15 gxh3 ♕f3+** (Adorjan – Parma, Moscow 1977). The text is a risky attempt to play for the win.

15   ...   ♖ae8
16   ♕xf8+   ♕xf8!

The correspondence game Yavorsky – Gartner, 1980/82 saw the weaker **16 ... ♖xf8?** 17 ♗a3 ♖e8 18 ♖af1 ♕xd2 19 gxh3 ♕a5 20 ♗d6±

17   ♖f1   ♗xg2+
18   ♔xg2

This is a critical position for the variation. Rabino-vitch – Zauerman, Correspondence 1981/86 saw the inferior **18   ...   ♕e7?** and after 19 ♗b2 ♕g5+ 20 ♔h1 c5 21 ♖f5 White had a winning position. Instead ...

18 ... ♕d6!

... is the right continuation, keeping counterchances - see illustrative game 6, Kalegin - Mik. Tseitlin.

B12

7 ♕e2 ♗e7

8 ♗xc6

8 0-0 0-0 (8 ... ♘d4 is examined above) 9 ♗xc6 leads to the main variation.

8 d3 ♘d4 9 ♘xd4 exd4 10 h4 h6 11 ♗d2 c6 12 ♗a4 ♔d8!? 13 0-0-0 a5 14 c4 dxc3∓ Korneyev - Mik. Tseitlin, Moscow 1976.

8 ... dxc6

Also worth attention is **8 ... bxc6.** Penrose - Boey, Lugano 1968 developed 9 ♕xe5 (9 d4 ♕g6! 10 dxe5 0-0 11 0-0 d6) 9 ... ♕f7 10 0-0 (taking the second pawn is dangerous, viz 10 ♕xc7 0-0 11 d3 {11 0-0 ♕g6 12 ♘e5 ♕e6} 11 ... ♕e6+ {11 ... ♗d8!?} 12 ♕e5 ♗b4+ 13 ♔f1 (13 c3 ♕g6) 13 ... ♕f7 14 a3 ♗e7 15 ♗g5 ♗xg5 16 ♕xg5 ♖b8 17 b3 ♖b5 18 ♕e3 ♖f5∓) 10 ... d6 11 ♕g3 0-0 12 d4? (more to the point are 12 d3 or 12 b3) 12 ... ♖b8 13 b3 ♖b5! 14 ♖e1? (after the text, White's position becomes critical, preferable is 14 ♗d2 ♕h5 15 ♖ae1 ♗d8 16 c4 ♖bf5 17 ♖e4= Palermo - Arjala, Finland 1975) 14 ... ♖f5 15 ♗e3 ♕h5! with very dangerous threats.

9 ♘xe5

9 d4 ♗g4 10 dxe5 ♕g6=
9 ♕xe5 ♗g4 10 ♕xf6 (10 d4 ♗xf3 11 gxf3 ♕xf3 12 ♖g1 0-0-0 13 ♗e3 ♗f6 14 ♕e6+ ♔b8 15 ♕g4 ♕d5∓ Orlov - Ivanov, Leningrad 1973) 10 ... ♗xf6

White's possibilities from this position:

a) **11 ♘g1** 0-0-0 12 f3 ♗f5 13 d3 ♖he8+ 14 ♘e2 ♖e7 15 ♔f2 (15 ♔d1 c5!) 15 ... ♖de8, and due to his lack of development White will have trouble defnding himself.

b) **11 0-0** 0-0-0 12 ♖e1 (12 d3 ♗xf3 13 gxf3 ♖he8) 12 ... ♖he8 13 ♖xe8 ♖xe8 14 ♔f1 ♗xf3 15 gxf3 ♕e5 16 h3 ♕f8 17 ♔g2 ♕f6 18 d3 ♕g6+ 19 ♔h1 ♕d4∓ Yadul - Ross, Correspondence 1975)

c) **11 d3** ♗xf3 (or 11 ... 0-0-0 and if 12 ♘g5 then 12 ... ♖he8+ 13 ♘e4 ♖xe4+!) 12 gxf3 0-0-0 13 ♖b1 ♖d5 14 ♗e3 ♖e8 15 ♔d2 ♖a5 16 a3 ♖h5 17 h3 ♖h4∓ Yusupov - Mik. Tseitlin, Rostov 1981)

d) **11 c3** c5 12 d3 0-0-0 13 ♔e2 ♖d5 (13 ... c4 14 dxc4 {14 d4 c5! gives Black good counterplay, e.g. 15 dxc5 ♗f5 16 ♗e3 ♗d3+ 17 ♔e1 ♖he8 18 ♘d4 ♗g5 19 ♔d2 ♗xe3+ 20 fxe3 ♖f8} 14 ... ♗e6 15 ♖d1 (15 ♗e3 ♗xc4+ 16 ♔e1 ♖d3) 15 ... ♗xc4+ 16 ♔e1 ♖xd1+ 17 ♔xd1 ♖d8+ 18 ♔e1 ♖d5 19 ♗d2 ♖a5 20 a3 ♖b5 21 b4 ♖d5 and despite the extra white pawn, Black's chances are better) 14 ♗e3 (Here ECO states that White's position is better)

14 ... ♖hd8 15 ♖ad1 ♗f5! 16 d4 c4 17 ♖d2 ♗d3+ 18 ♔d1 ♖a5∞ Mik. Tseitlin - Arbakov, Moscow 1988.

Returning to the main variation after 9 ♘xe5:

9   ...   ♗f5

Also possible is **9 ... 0-0!?** 10 0-0 ♗d6 11 ♘c4 (11 d4 ♗f5! 12 f4 ♗xe5 13 dxe5 ♕g6 14 ♖f2 ♖ad8 15 ♗e3 a5 with good positional compensation for the pawn, Morozov - Mik. Tseitlin, Correspondence 1985/87) 11 ... ♕g6 12 ♘xd6 cxd6 with good piece play.

10   d3

Weaker is **10 c3** 0-0-0 11 0-0 c5 12 f4 ♖he8 13 d3 ♕a6 14 ♖d1 ♗f6.

10 d4 0-0! leads to Morozov - Tseitlin above, but in the correspondence game Levin - Banfalvi (1985/89) Black chose instead 10 ... 0-0-0 11 ♗e3

♗d6 12 f4 ♗xe5 13 dxe5! (13 fxe5 ♕g6 14 c3 ♖he8) 13 ... ♕h4+? (better 13 ... ♕g6) and after 14 ♕f2! ♕xf2+ 15 ♔xf2 ♗xc2 16 h3 h5 17 g4 ♗e4 18 ♖hd1 hxg4 19 ♖xd8+ ♔xd8 20 hxg4 White had the advantage.

10 ...   0-0!

Lyavdansky recommends 10 ... 0-0-0 but this seems weaker after 11 0-0! ♖he8 (11 ... ♗d6 12 ♘c4! ♖hf8 13 ♗e3! △ ♖ab1 & b4↑) 12 f4 (also good is 12 ♘c4 ♗c5 13 ♗e3 ♕g6 14 ♕f3) 12 ... ♗d6 (12 ... g5 13 ♕f2) 13 ♕f2 (13 ♕f3!?) 13 ... ♔b8 14 ♗e3 a6 15 ♗d4 ♕f8 16 ♘c4 ♗c8 17 a3! g6 18 b4 ♕h6 19 ♗c5 ♗e6 20 ♗xd6 cxd6 21 ♘a5± Glek - Arbakov, Sochi 1985.

11   0-0

11 ♗d2 ♗d6 12 ♗c3 ♖ae8 13 f4 ♕h4+ 14 ♕f2 (14 g3 ♕h3 15 ♔d2 ♗xe5 16 ♗xe5 ♗g4 17 ♕f1 ♕h5∓) 14 ... ♕xf2+ 15 ♔xf2 ♗xe5 16 ♗xe5 ♗xd3=

11   ...   ♖ae8

see following diagram

In this position, Black has definite compensation for the sacrificed pawn.

12   d4

12 ♘c4 ♕g6 13 ♔h1 ♗c5 14 ♗e3 b5 15 ♕d2 ♗e7 16 ♘e5

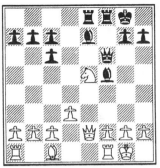

♕f6 17 f4 ♗d6 (17 ... c5) 18 d4 ♗xe5 (18 ... ♗e4) 19 dxe5 (after 19 fxe5! White would have the better chances) 19 ... ♕g6 20 c3 ♗e4 21 ♖ad1 ♕g4∓ Silva - Mik. Tseitlin, Odessa 1976.

12   ...   ♗d6
13   f4   ♗xe5
14   dxe5   ♕g6
15   ♖f2   h5

15 ... ♖d8 16 ♗e3 ♖d5 (16 ... a5 17 ♔h1 h5 18 h3 ♖d5 19 ♖c1 ♖fd8 20 ♖ff1 b6 21 ♕f2 c5 22 ♔h2 ♖f8 23 ♖fe1 ♗e4 24 ♕e2 ♗f5 25 ♖f1 ♖fd8 26 ♕f2 ♖f8∞ Schlosser - Outerello, European Team Ch, Haifa 1989) 17 a4 a5 18 ♖af1 h5 19 ♔h1 h4 20 h3 ♖fd8∞ Marjanovic - Vilmas, Kavala 1985.

16   ♗e3

Kindermann - Kotronias, Dortmund 1989 offered further evidence that Black has no need to be afraid of this position, e.g. 16 ♔h1 ♖d8 17 ♗e3 ♖d5 18 h3 ♖fd8 19 ♖e1 b6 20 ♔h2 ♗f7 21 ♖f3 h4 22 ♗f2 ♖d2 23 ♕c4+ ♗e6 24 ♕xc6 ♖xc2 25 f5 ♖xc6 26 fxg6+ ♔xg6 27 ♖e2 ♗xa2 28 ♗xh4 ♖e8 29 ♖a3 ½-½.

16	...	b6
17	b4	h4
18	♖e1	♖e6
19	♗d4	♖d8
20	c3	♕e8
21	♕f3	♖g6
22	♖d2	♕e6
23	♕d1	h3
24	g3	♕f7
25	♕b3	

Unzicker - Mik. Tseitlin, Moscow 1982, and now ...

| 25 | ... | ♗e6! |

... keeps the balance.

B2

6	♕e2

Here we analyse the consequences of Black's two responses:

B21) 6 ... ♕e7
B22) 6 ... d5

In the event of 6 ... ♗e7, 7 ♘g3! leads to a favourable variation from the game Kupurosov - Jandemirov – see variation A, note to White's sixth.

B21

6	...	♕e7

7	0-0

Others are not dangerous for Black:

a) 7 ♗xc6 bxc6 (7 ... dxc6 8 d3 ♗g4 9 h3 ♗h5 10 ♘g3 ♗xf3 11 ♕xf3 0-0-0= Shishov - Mik. Tseitlin, Moscow 1977) 8 d4 ♘xe4 9 ♕xe4 exd4 10 ♕xe7+ ♗xe7 11 ♘xd4 ♗f6∓ Ghitescu - Letelier, Leipzig 1960.

b) 7 c4 ♘d4 8 ♘xf6+ gxf6 9 ♘xd4 exd4 10 ♕xe7+ ♗xe7 11 0-0 ♔f7 12 ♗a4 d6 13 ♗d1 h5= Kirpichnikov - Lanka,

Riga 1977.

c) **7 c3** d5 8 ♘xf6+ gxf6 9 d4 exd4 10 ♘xd4 ♕xe2+ 11 ♘xe2 ♗e6 12 ♘f4 ♗f7 ½ : ½ Balashov - Bronstein, Moscow 1978.

d) **7 d3** d6 8 ♗g5 (8 0-0 ♗d7 9 ♗e3 a6 10 ♗a4 b5 11 ♗b3 ♘a5 12 ♗d2 ♘xb3 13 axb3 ♗c6 14 c4 ♘xe4 15 dxe4 ♕d7 16 ♘g5 ♗e7 17 f4 ♗xg5 18 fxg5 ♖f8∓ Tal - Mik. Tseitlin, Moscow 1982) 8 ... ♗d7 9 0-0-0 0-0-0 10 ♔b1 h6 11 ♘xf6 gxf6 12 ♗h4 ♖g8∓ Fatalibekova - Mik. Tseitlin, Moscow 1975.

7 ... d5

8 ♘g3

8 ♘c3 ♗g4! 9 ♕xe5 ♗xf3 10 ♕xe7+ ♗xe7 11 ♗xc6+ bxc6 12 gxf3 0-0∞

On 8 ♘xf6+ Black should answer 8 ... gxf6 9 d4 e4 with the following possibilities:

a) **10 ♘h4** f5! 11 g3 (11 ♗xc6+ bxc6 12 ♕h5+ ♕f7 13 ♕xf7+ ♔xf7 14 f3 ♗g7 15 c3 ♗f6!∓) 11 ... ♗g7 12 ♗xc6+ bxc6 13 c3 0-0 14 ♘g2 a5!=

b) **10 ♘d2** ♗d7 (also possible is 10 ... ♗g7!? 11 f3 {11 c4 0-0 and 11 ♕h5+ ♕f7 are favourable for Black} 11 ... 0-0 12 ♗xc6 bxc6 13 fxe4 ♖e8 14 ♖e1 ♗f5 15 ♕a6 and now Black can choose bet-

ween 15 ... ♕d7, 15 ... ♕d6 and 15 ... c5!? with good counterplay) 11 c4 0-0-0 12 ♘b3 ♖g8 13 ♗f4 dxc4 14 ♗xc4 ♖g4 15 ♗g3 f5. Shashin - Ivanov, Leningrad 1963 now continued 16 f3 exf3 17 ♕xf3 ♘xd4 18 ♘xd4 ♖xd4 19 ♖ac1, and with 19 ... ♗c6! 20 ♕xf5+ ♔b8 Black could get good counterplay.

Returning to the main line after 8 ♘g3

8 ... e4

Black's other possibility is **8 ... ♗g4** which involves a pawn sacrifice. Tseshkovsky - Bronstein, Vilnius 1975 continued 9 ♕xe5 (9 d3 0-0-0) 9 ... ♗xf3 10 ♕xe7+ (Bronstein recommends 10 ♕c3! as White's best. After 10 ... ♗xg2 11 ♗xc6+ bxc6 12 ♕xc6+ ♔f7 13 ♔xg2! ♖b8 14 d3 ♖b6 15 ♕c3 ♕d7 16 ♗g5 ♗e7 Black still has to prove the correctness of the pawn sacrifice) 10 ... ♔xe7! 11 ♗xc6 bxc6 12 gxf3 ♔d7 13 d3 ♗d6 14 ♗d2 ♖hf8 15 f4 ♘g8! 16 ♗c3 and now Black had the straightforward possibility of 16 ... ♖f7! 17 f5 ♘e7 returning a pawn to get the better position.

9   ♘d4   ♗d7
10   ♗xc6

10 ♘xc6 bxc6 11 ♗a4 h5 12 ♖e1 h4 13 ♘f1 ♔f7 (better is 13 ... h3! at once) 14 d3 exd3 15 ♕d1 ♕b4 16 cxd3 h3∓

10   ...   bxc6
11   d3

11   ...   c5!

11 ... ♕e5 12 ♘f3! ♕e7 13 dxe4 dxe4 (13 ... ♘xe4 14 ♘xe4) 14 ♘g5 and 15 ♕c4±

11 ... exd3 12 ♕xd3 ♕b4 13 c3 ♕c4 14 ♖e1+ ♔f7 15 ♕c2± Nicevsky – Mik. Tseitlin, Nalencow 1979.

12   ♘df5

12 ♘b3 exd3 13 ♕xe7+ ♗xe7 14 cxd3 (Alexandria

– Levitina, Moscow 1975) and now Black has various methods of obtaining a good position:

a) **14 ... a5** 15 ♗e3 d4 16 ♗g5 a4 17 ♘d2 h6

b) **14 ... ♗a4** 15 ♗e3 ♗xb3 16 axb3 ♔f7 17 d4 (17 ♘f5 d4! 18 ♗g5 ♖hb8) 17 ... cxd4 18 ♗xd4 c5

c) **14 ... ♗b5!** 15 ♖d1 0-0-0.

12   ...   ♗xf5

Others:

a) **12 ... ♕e5** 13 dxe4 ♘xe4 (13 ... dxe4 14 f4 {14 ♕a6!?} 14 ... ♕d5 15 ♘e3 ♕b7 16 ♘c4 △ 17 ♘e5±) 14 f3! ♗xf5 15 ♘xf5 ♕xf5 16 fxe4 ♕xe4 17 ♕b5+±

b) **12 ... ♕e6** 13 dxe4 ♘xe4 (13 ... dxe4 14 f3 exf3 15 ♕xf3 ♗c6 16 ♕c3) 14 ♘xe4 ♕xe4 (14 ... dxe4 15 ♘g3 ♗c6 16 f3 and Black loses a pawn without getting any counterplay) 15 ♕xe4+ dxe4 16 ♘g3 ♗c6 17 ♖e1 0-0-0 18 ♗f4! ♗d6 19 ♗xd6 ♖xd6 20 ♘xe4 ♗xe4 21 ♖xe4 ♖d2 22 ♖c4±

13   ♘xf5   ♕e6

see following diagram

This position can be reasonably assessed as dynamically equal. We will now follow the game Don-

chenko - Mik. Tseitlin, Moscow 1975.

14 dxe4

The retreat of the knight with **14 ♘g3** should not concern Black if he continues actively, e.g. 14 ... ♗d6 15 dxe4 ♗xg3 16 fxg3 (16 hxg3 0-0 17 e5 ♘e4∓) 16 ... 0-0 17 ♗f4 ♖f7 (17 ... c6) 18 e5 ♘e4 and the black initiative gives sufficient compensation for the pawn.

14	...	♕xe4
15	♕b5+	♔f7
16	♕b7	♕xf5!?

16 ... ♖d8=

16 ... ♗e7 17 ♘xe7 ♕xe7 18 ♗f4 ♖hb8=

17	♕xa8	♖g8
18	♕xa7	♗d6

With a strong attack in return for the sacrificed exchange.

B22

6	...	d5

This continuation gives Black good counterplay.

7 ♘xf6+

There is no convenient retreat for the knight. For example:

a) 7 ♘eg5 ♗d6 8 ♘xe5 0-0 9 ♘xc6 bxc6 10 ♗xc6 ♖b8 11 ♘e6 (11 c3 ♖b6 12 ♗a4 ♗f4 13 d4 ♘g4! 14 ♗xf4 ♖xf4 15 ♕e8+ ♕xe8+ 16 ♗xe8 h6-+ Shlekis - Normantas, Vilnius 1979) 11 ... ♗xe6 12 ♕xe6+ ♔h8 13 ♕h3 ♖b6 14 ♗a4 ♖b4↑ Huld - End, Stockholm 1972.

b) 7 ♘g3 ♗d6 (also very acceptable for Black is 7 ... e4 8 ♘d4 ♗d7 9 ♗xc6 bxc6 10 d3 ♗c5 11 ♘b3 ♗d6 12 dxe4 0-0 13 exd5 ♘xd5 Ivanovic - Tatai, Stip 1979) 8 ♘xe5 0-0 9 ♘xc6 (9 ♗xc6 bxc6 10 ♘xc6? {preferable is 10 d4 c5 11 c3 cxd4 12 cxd4 c5 but Black is developing a pleasant initiative} 10 ... ♕d7 11 ♕b5 a6 12 ♕a4 ♗b7 and White is left a piece down) 9 ... bxc6 10 ♗xc6 ♖b8 11 0-0 (11 d3 ♖b6 12 ♗a4 ♖b4 13 b3 ♖xa4! 14 bxa4 ♖e8 15 ♗e3 d4 and White faces material loss) 11 ... ♖b6 12 ♗a4 ♘g4! 13 d4 ♘xh2! 14 ♔xh2 ♕h4+ 15 ♔g1 ♗a6∓ Shutt - Gunter, Correspondence 1970/71.

c) 7 ♘xe5 dxe4 8 ♕c4 ♕d5 9 ♕xd5 ♘xd5 10 ♘xc6 ♗d7 11 ♘d4 c6 12 ♗c4 ♗c5! 13 ♗xd5 (13 ♘e2 ♖f8 14 0-0 0-0-0 15 d4 exd3 16 ♗xd3 {16 cxd3 ♗g4} 16 ... ♖xf2 △ ... ♖f8 and Black restores the material balance while keeping the initiative) 13 ... cxd5 14 ♘b3 ♗b6 15 0-0 0-0∓

7 ... gxf6
8 d4 ♗g7!

This active defence was only discovered recently. The old continuation was in White's favour, e.g. **8 ... e4** 9 ♘h4 (9 ♘e5 fxe5 10 ♕h5+ ♔d7 11 ♕xe5∞) 9 ... ♕e7 10 ♗f4! ♗e6 (weaker is 10 ... f5 11 g3! ♗g7 as after 12 ♕h5+ ♕f7 13 ♕xf7+ ♔xf7 14 c3 Black is left a pawn down) 11 0-0 (11 g3 a6 12 ♗xc6+ bxc6 13 ♗h6± Monticelli - Spielmann, Warsaw 1935) 11 ... ♕d7 12 f3! exf3 13 ♖xf3

♔d8 (13 ... 0-0-0 14 ♗xc6 ♕xc6? 15 ♖c3) 14 ♕f2 ♗g7 15 ♖e1 ♖e8 16 c3 ♔c8 17 ♘d3!± Persidsky - Jorgenson, Correspondence 1979/80.

9 dxe5

9 c4 a6 10 ♗a4 ♗g4 11 dxe5 0-0 12 cxd5 ♘xe5 13 ♗e3 (13 ♗b3 ♖e8 14 ♗e3 f5∓) 13 ... c5 14 ♗b3 ♖c8 15 ♖c1 f5 16 0-0 (16 h3? ♗xf3 17 gxf3 f4 and Black is better as 18 ♗xc5? runs into 18 ... ♕a5+) 16 ... ♕e8!? 17 d6+ ♔h8 18 ♖fe1 (18 ... f4 was threatened) 18 ... ♗xf3 19 gxf3 ♕h5 20 ♗d5 b6 21 ♖cd1 (21 ♗f4 ♘g6 22 ♕d2 ♗d4!?∞) 21 ... ♖cd8 22 ♗f4 ♘g6 reaching a sharp position with approximately equal chances, Mortensen - Wedberg, Copenhagen 1983.

9 ... 0-0
10 exf6

10 ♗xc6 bxc6 is not worrying for Black. Nenashev - Arbakov, Moscow 1986 continued 11 e6 ♖e8 12 0-0 c5! (delaying the capture on e6 and maintaining flexibility is a very accurate way to play. 12 ... ♗xe6 proved to be less precise, but quite playable in Ochoa - Chiburdanidze, Bilbao 1987 - 13 ♘d4 ♕d6 14 ♕f3 ♕d8 15 ♕e2 ♗f7 16 ♕f3 ♗g6

17 ♘f5 ½-½) 13 ♕b5 (13 c4
♕d6! 14 ♖d1 ♖xe6 15 ♕c2 d4
16 b4 ♗b7∓) 13 ... ♗f8 14
♗e3 (14 ♗f4 ♗xe6 15 ♖fe1
½-½ Sax - Chandler, Hastings 1990/91) 14 ... d4 15
♖fd1 ♗d6 16 ♗xd4 cxd4 17
♘xd4 ♗xe6 18 ♘xe6 ♖xe6=
11 ♗f4 seems to be an inferior alternative to 11 e6,
e.g. 11 ... ♖e8 (11 ... fxe5 12
♗g5 ♕d6 13 c3 ♕g6 14 h4
♗g4 15 ♕d2 ♕e4+-+ Rosch -
Ebeling, Argentina 1935) 12
0-0-0 fxe5 13 ♗e3 (13 ♗xe5
♗g4; 13 ♘xe5 ♕f6) 13 ... ♕d6
14 c3 ♗g4 15 h3 ♗xf3 16
♕xf3 ♖ab8 17 ♕g3 ♔h8∓
Huski - Vindenmann, Correspondence 1980/82.

10 e6 is well met by 10 ...
♘e5! There are many examples of this, all of which
bear out this assessment,
e.g.

a) **11 ♕d1** ♗xe6 12 ♘d4
♗c8 13 ♗e2 c5 14 ♘b3 b6 15
c3 f5 16 0-0 ♗b7 and Black's
superiority is not in question, Mokry - Mik. Tseitlin,
Prague 1985.

b) **11 0-0** c6 12 ♗a4 (12
♗d3 simply provided further evidence of Black's
superiority here, e.g. 12 ...
♗xe6 13 ♘d4 ♗g4 14 f3 ♗d7
15 ♘f5 ♘xd3 16 ♕xd3 ♕b6+
17 ♔h1 ♗xf5 18 ♕xf5 ♖ae8 19

♗f4 ♖e2 20 b3 ♖fe8 21 h4
♕b4 22 ♖fd1 ♕c5 23 ♖d2
♖xd2 24 ♗xd2 ♕d4 25 ♖d1
♕xh4+ 26 ♔g1 ♖e2 27 ♕g4
♕f2+ 28 ♔h1 f5 29 ♕g5 h6
0-1 Renet - Mik. Tseitlin,
Palma Open 1989) 12 ... ♗xe6
13 ♘d4 ♗d7 14 f4 ♕b6 15 c3
Popovic - Kurajica, Sarajevo
1985. Kurajica now played
the inferior 15 ... ♗g4?! but
after 16 ♕c2 ♘c4 17 f5 ♖fe8
18 ♕f2 ♗e2 19 ♖e1 ♗d3 20
♖e6 ♖xe6 21 fxe6 ♖e8 22 b3
♘e5 23 ♗f4 ♗g6 24 ♔h1 ♕a6
went on to win anyway.
Much better would have
been 15 ... ♖ae8 with a decisive advantage.

c) **11 ♗e3** c6 12 ♗d3 ♗xe6
13 ♘d4 ♗g4 14 f3 ♗d7 15
♘b3 b6 16 ♗a6 ♖e8 17 0-0
♗c8 18 ♖fe1 ♗xa6 19 ♕xa6
♕c8 20 ♕xc8 ♖axc8 21 ♖ad1
♘c4 22 ♗c1 f5 23 ♖xe8+
♖xe8 24 c3 a5 and Black
eventually triumphed in the
endgame Tseshkovsky -
Yilmaz, Kusadasi Open 1990

d) **11 ♗f4** ♘g6 (11 ... ♕d6
12 0-0 ♕xe6 13 ♖ae1 c6 14
♗d3 ♘xd3 15 ♕xd3 ♕f7 16
♗d6 ♖d8 17 ♕a3 ♗e6 18 ♘d4
♖e8 19 ♖e3 ♕d7 20 ♖fe1 ♗f7
21 h3 ♖xe3 22 ♖xe3 ♖e8 ½-½
Hellers - Antunes, Novi
Sad Olympiad 1990) 12 e7
♘xe7 13 0-0-0 ♘g6 14 ♗e3

c6 15 ♗d3 ♛a5 16 ♚b1 c5 17
c4 d4 18 ♗d2 ♛c7 19 ♗e4
♘f4 20 ♗xf4 ♛xf4 21 ♛d3
f5 22 ♗d5+ ♚h8 23 ♖de1 ♗d7
24 g3 ♛h6 25 h4 ♗f6 26 ♘e5
♗xe5 27 ♖xe5 ♖ae8 and was
drawn in fifty moves, Wedberg – Hynes, Novi Sad Olympiad 1990.

10	...	♛xf6
11	♛d1	♘d4

Also very good is 11 ...
♗g4!? e.g.

a) 12 ♗e2 ♖ae8 13 0-0
♖xe2! 14 ♛xe2 ♘d4 15 ♛d3
♗xf3 16 gxf3 ♘xf3+ 17 ♚g2
♘e1+ and the rest is a mopping up operation.

b) 12 ♛xd5+ ♚h8 13 0-0
♖ad8! 14 ♛g5 ♗xf3 15 ♛xf6
♖xf6 16 gxf3 ♘d4 with a
clear advantage.

12	♛xd4	♛e7+

see following diagram

13	♘e5	

13 ♛e3 is well met by 13
... ♛b4+ 14 c3 ♛xb5.

13	...	♗xe5
14	♛xd5+	♚h8
15	♗e2	♗g4

16	♗e3	

16 ♛c4 ♗xe2 17 ♛xe2
♖ae8 18 ♗e3 ♗xb2.

16	...	♗xe2
17	♚xe2	♗xb2
18	♖ad1	♖ae8
19	♖d3	

... ♖xf2+ was a threat.

19	...	c6
20	♛c4	

20 ♛d6 ♛g7.

The text is following
Klovan – Arbakov, 1984.
Here Black should have
continued

20	...	♛g5!
21	♚d1	

21 g3 ♛h5+

21	...	♛xg2
22	♗d4+	♗xd4
23	♛xd4+	♛g7=

8) 4 ♘c3 fxe4 5 ♘xe4 d5

1	e4	e5
2	♘f3	♘c6
3	♗b5	f5
4	♘c3	fxe4
5	♘xe4	d5

This heavily analysed continuation leads to sharp play and demands good theoretical knowledge from both White and Black. During recent years, its reputation has suffered and it has not been seen too frequently, attention having transferred to 5 ... ♘f6. This, in our opinion, is unjust.

In this chapter, we examine the knight retreat 6 ♘g3. The more aggressive 6 ♘xe5 will be the subject of chapter nine.

6 ♘g3 does not mount an immediate challenge the Black centre, and also puts the knight slightly out of play. Nevertheless, White has a development advantage and Black must be careful not to let this turn into a full scale assault against his central installations.

The other alternative, 6 ♘c3 is harmless allowing Black easy counterplay, e.g. 6 ... ♗g4! 7 ♕e2 ♗xf3 8 ♕xe5+ ♔f7 (also fine is 8 ... ♕e7 9 ♕xe7+ ♘gxe7 10 gxf3 0-0-0 11 ♘e2 ♘e5 12 ♘d4 ♘7g6∞) 9 ♗xc6 bxc6 10 ♕f4+ ♘f6 11 ♕xf3 ♗d6 12 0-0 ♖f8 13 d4 ♔g8 14 ♕h3 ♕e8∞

6 ♘g3

6 ...   ♗g4

Of the other possible Black responses, only **6 ... ♕d6!?**, which Nikitin offers without analysis, seems worthy of attention. Practical experience of the alternatives is not encouraging:

a) 6 ... ♕f6 7 d4 e4 8 ♘e5 ♗d6 9 ♘xc6 ♗d7 10 ♕h5+ g6 11 ♕xd5 bxc6 12 ♕xe4+ ♔f8 13 ♗e2 ♖e8 14 ♕d3 ♕h4 15 ♗d2 ♘f6 16 0-0-0± Vasyukov – Bonch-Osmolovsky, Moscow 1961.

b) 6 ... ♗d6 7 ♘xe5 ♘ge7 (7 ... ♗xe5 8 ♗xc6+ bxc6 9 ♕h5+) 8 ♗xc6+ bxc6 9 d4 0-0 10 0-0 with a sound extra pawn, Stromberg – Guggenburger, Buenos Aires 1978.

c) 6 ... e4 7 ♘d4! ♕d6 (7 ... ♕f6 8 ♕h5+ ♔e7 9 ♘df5+ ♔e6 was refuted in neat fashion in Moiseev – Ivanov, Baku 1985 viz 10 ♗xc6! bxc6 11 ♕e8+ ♘e7 12 ♘xe7 ♗xe7 13 ♕xc6+ ♔e5 14 f4+!) 8 d3 exd3 (8 ... ♘f6 9 dxe4 dxe4 10 ♘xc6) 9 ♕xd3 ♘ge7 (better is 9 ... ♗d7 10 0-0 0-0-0 11 ♗xc6 ♗xc6 12 ♗g5 ♘f6 13 ♘gf5 ♕d7 14 ♖fe1± Nevednichy – Gipslis, 1964) 10 0-0 ♗d7 11 ♗xc6! bxc6 (11 ... ♗xc6 12 ♘gf5 ♕d7 13 ♗g5!) 12 ♖e1 g6 13 ♘b3 h5 14

♕d4 ♖h7 15 ♗f4 and White won in the correspondence game Ekstrom – Stromberg, 1964.

7   h3

Black is not troubled by the alternatives:

7 0-0 ♕f6! The pressure that this generates against f3 should be sufficient to alleviate any opening difficulties. For example 8 ♖e1 ♘ge7 9 d4 0-0-0 10 ♗g5 ♗xf3 11 ♗xf6 ♗xd1 12 ♗xe7 ♘xe7 13 ♖axd1 a6= Mortensen – Tukmakov, Reykjavik 1990.

7 ♕e2 ♗d6 8 d4 e4! 9 h3 (9 c4 ♔f8!) 9 ... ♗d7 10 ♘e5 ♘xd4

7 d3 ♗d6 (7 ... ♕d6!?)

7 d4 also promises little, although it is more complex, e.g. 7 ... e4 (7 ... exd4 8 0-0 ♗e7 leads to a position from chapter seven) 8 h3 exf3 (8 ... ♗d7 9 ♗xc6 ♗xc6!

{also perfectly playable is 9 ... bxc6 10 ♘e5 ♘f6 11 ♘h5 g6 12 ♘xf6+ ♕xf6 13 0-0 ♗d6 14 ♗e3 ♕e6 15 f4 0-0 16 c4 ♖ab8 17 ♕e2 ♖b4 18 c5 ♗e7 19 ♔h1 ♗f6 20 ♖ab1 ♖fb8 21 b3 a5 22 ♕c2 ♗c8 23 a3 ♖4b5 and Black went on to convert his advantage in Panchenko - Sekulic, Belgrade 1989} 10 ♘e5 ♘f6=) 9 hxg4 fxg2 and now:

a) **10 ♗xc6+** bxc6 11 ♕e2+ ♕e7=

b) **10 ♕e2+** ♔f7!? 11 ♕f3+ ♕f6 12 ♕xg2 (12 ♕xd5+ ♕e6+ 13 ♕xe6+ ♔xe6 14 ♖g1 ♘xd4∓) 12 ... ♕xd4 13 ♕f3+ ♘f6! 14 ♗xc6 bxc6 15 g5 ♕g4∓ Shusterman - Gusev, Moscow 1968)

c) **10 ♖g1** ♕d6 (10 ... ♕e7+ 11 ♕e2 ♕xe2+ 12 ♔xe2 0-0-0 13 ♗e3 ♘f6 14 ♔f3 h5 15 gxh5 ♘xh5 16 ♘xh5 ♖xh5 17 ♖xg2 ♖d6= Kupreichik - Barreras, Plovdiv 1980) 11 ♕e2+ ♘ge7 12 ♗g5 0-0-0 13 0-0-0 h6 (Shusterman - Agzamov, Moscow 1966) and now after 14 ♗xc6 ♕xc6 15 ♗xe7 ♖e8 16 ♘f5 g6 17 ♕f3 as recommended by Schwarz, the chances are approximately equal.

7   ...   ♗xf3
8   ♕xf3   ♘f6

In our opinion 8 ... ♕d6!?

also solves Black's problems. This alternative to the text has been the subject of some recent attention and practical results bear out our assessment. Witness the following material:

a) **9 ♘f5** ♕e6 10 ♕g4 ♔f7 11 ♘e3 ♘f6 12 ♕xe6+ ♔xe6 13 0-0 ♘d4 14 ♗a4 b5 15 ♗b3 a5∓ Camilleri - Boey, Nice 1974.

b) **9 c3** 0-0-0 (9 ... e4 is perhaps slightly inferior to the text, but nevertheless left Black with no problems in Balashov - Kuzmin, Moscow 1989, e.g. 10 ♕e2 0-0-0 11 0-0 a6 12 ♗xc6 ♕xc6 13 d3 exd3 14 ♕xd3 ♘f6 15 ♗g5 ♗c5 16 b4 ♗b6 17 ♘f5 ♖d7 18 a4 ♕c4 19 ♖ad1 ♕xd3 20 ♖xd3 ♘e4 21 ♗e3 ♗xe3 22 ♖xe3 g6 23 ♘d4 c5 24 ♘e6 cxb4 25 cxb4 ♔b8 26 f3 ♘g3 and was eventually

drawn after 61 moves) 10
0-0 ♔b8 11 d4 e4 12 ♕d1 g6
13 ♗g5 ♗e7 14 ♗e3 h5 15 ♕d2
h4 16 ♘e2 ♘f6∓ Kurajica -
Tatai, Karlovac 1979.

c) **9 0-0** 0-0-0 10 ♘f5
(Others also fail to make
an impression on the black
position, e.g. 10 ♗xc6 ♕xc6!
11 ♕f5+ ♔b8 12 ♕xe5 ♕xc2
or 10 c3 ♘f6 11 d4 exd4 12
♘f5 ♕c5 13 ♗xc6 ♕xc6 14
♘xd4 ♕d7 15 ♗g5 ♗c5=
Smirin - Tukmakov, Lvov
1990) 10 ... ♕c5 11 ♗xc6
♕xc6 12 d4 e4= Djuric -
Tatai, Vrnjacka Banja 1979.

d) 9 c4 0-0-0 10 ♗xc6
♕xc6 11 cxd5 ♕xd5 12 ♕xd5
♖xd5 13 ♔e2 ♘e7 gives
Black a perfectly accept-
able endgame. Akopian -
Kuzmin, Podolsk 1990 con-
tinued 14 d3 ♘c6 15 ♗e3 ♗c5
16 ♖hd1 ♖hd8 17 ♘e4 ♗b6 18
♘c3 ♖5d6 19 ♘e4 ♖d5 20
♘c3 ♖5d7 21 a3 ♘d4+ 22
♗xd4 ♗xd4 23 ♖d2 a6 24
♘e4 ♖d5 and was eventual-
ly drawn.

The above lines serve to
demonstrate that 8 ... ♕d6
is a perfectly feasible alternative to the main lines
with 8 ... ♘f6. The Black
play is also consistent with
the themes of this variation
and will repay study.

In this position White
has a wide choice. We shall
examine in detail the following:

A) 9 c4
B) 9 0-0
C) 9 ♘h5

Others:

a) **9 d3** ♕d6 (9 ... ♗d6! 10
♘h5 0-0 11 ♘xf6+ ♕xf6 12
♕xf6 {12 ♕xd5+ ♔h8 13 0-0
♘d4 doesn't help} 12 ...
gxf6∓ Mik. Tseitlin - Kupreichik, Minsk 1969) 10 0-0
0-0-0 11 ♗xc6 ♕xc6 12 ♗g5
h6 13 ♗xf6 gxf6 14 c4 dxc4
15 ♕xc6 bxc6 16 dxc4 ♖d4
with good play, Ravinsky -
Bronstein, Moscow 1954.

b) **9 ♕c3** ♕d6 10 ♗xc6+
♕xc6 11 ♕xc6+ (11 ♕xe5+
♔f7 12 ♕f5 ♖e8+ is risky for
White) 11 ... bxc6 12 d3 ♗d6
13 ♗d2 0-0 14 0-0 ♘d7!=
Fuchs - Liebert, Berlin 1966.

c) **9 d4** e4 10 ♕c3 (10 ♕f5 ♗d6 11 ♗g5 {11 ♘h5 0-0 12 ♘xf6+ ♕xf6 13 ♕xd5+ ♔h8} 11 ... 0-0 12 ♗xf6 ♗b4+ 13 c3 ♖xf6∓) 10 ... ♕d7 11 a3 ♗d6 12 ♗g5 0-0 13 0-0 a6 14 ♗xc6 bxc6 and Black's chances are preferable, Resnichek – Vanka, Brno 1982.

d) **9 ♗xc6+** bxc6 10 ♕c3 ♕d6 11 0-0 ♔d7 (11 ... ♔f7 12 d4 exd4 13 ♕f3 {13 ♕xd4 ♕b4} 13 ... g6 or 13 ... ♖e8 and Black has good chances) 12 d4 ♖e8 13 ♗e3 (Tseshkovsky – Menvielle, Las Palmas 1976) and now 13 ... ♕b4! would have been equal.

A

9   c4

9   ...   ♔f7

Black, by threatening 10 ... ♘d4 forces the exchange of the 'Spanish' bishop. This move may look strange, but it is consistent with Black's policy of protecting the centre. It is instructive to compare this with variation C where Black also tolerates a certain amount of discomfort with his king in return for securing the centre.

However, there are other ways to play:

a) **9 ... e4** 10 ♕e2 ♗c5 11 d4 ♗b4+ 12 ♔f1 ♗e7! 13 ♘f5 g6 14 ♘xe7 ♔xe7 15 ♗e3 a6 16 ♗xc6 bxc6 17 ♖c1 ♕d6 18 c5 ♕e6= Nordstrom – Geransson, correspondence 1965. Instead of 10 ... ♗c5, Euwe recommends 10 ... ♗e7 with the following possibilities: 11 cxd5 ♕xd5; 11 ♘f5 0-0 12 cxd5 ♘b4; 11 0-0 0-0 or finally 11 d4 ♗b4+ (11 ... 0-0 or (11 ... exd3!? 12 ♕xd3 0-0 also come into consideration) with interesting complications.

b) **9 ... a6** (a suggestion of B. Nesterenko) when:

10 ♗xc6+ bxc6 11 0-0 ♗d6

10 cxd5 ♕xd5 11 ♕xd5 ♘xd5

and

10 ♗a4 b5 11 cxb5 ♘d4 12 bxa6+ c6

are all worthy of attention.

c) **9 ... ♗c5!?** seeking to increase the pressure against f2.

10	♗xc6	bxc6
11	0-0	♗d6

11 ... ♗c5 12 d3 ♖f8 13 ♗e3 ♗xe3 14 fxe3± (Keres).

12	d3	♖b8!
13	b3	♖e8
14	♗e3	a5
15	c5?!	

15	...	♗f8!

15 ... e4? 16 dxe4 ♗xg3 17 fxg3 ♖xe4 18 ♗g5± Beisser - Hajek, correspondence 1967. After the text, there is no reason for Black not to face the future with confidence.

16	♘h5	

16 ♗g5 h6!

16	...	♔g8
17	♗g5	♗e7

With the prospect of exchanges looming up, Black can count on excellent chances.

B

9   0-0

9	...	♗d6

For **9 ... ♗e7** see chapter seven, part A.

9 ... ♕d6 10 d4 e4 11 ♕f5 g6 12 ♕e5+ ♔f7 13 ♕xd6 ♗xd6= Richardson - Boey, correspondence 1972/76.

10	♘h5	

We now have the further dichotomy:

B1) 10 ... ♘h5
B2) 10 ... e4!

B1

10	...	♘xh5
11	♕xh5+	g6
12	♕f3	

see following diagram

12	...	a6

12 ... e4 is weak, e.g. 13 ♕c3 ♔d7 14 d3 ♕e7 15 dxe4 ♗b4 16 ♕b3 dxe4 17 ♗g5±

Konyukov – Ivanov, Moscow 1963.

13 ♘a4

The exchange **13 ♗xc6+** bxc6 serves only to strengthen Black's pawn centre. Ignatiev – Pismenny, Moscow 1964 continued 14 d4 (14 d3 ♕d7! 15 ♗h6 ♕f5 16 ♕e2 0-0-0 △ ... g5∓, Euwe) 14 ... e4 15 ♕c3 ♔d7 16 b4 ♕h4 17 a4 ♖hf8 18 ♗d2 g5 19 b5 axb5 20 axb5 cxb5 21 ♖xa8 ♖xa8 22 ♕e3 ♕f4∓

13 ... ♕h4
14 c4 ♕xc4

14 ... e4 15 ♕b3 0-0 (15 ... 0-0-0) 16 c5!±

15 ♕f6

see following diagram

15 ♗b3 ♕e4 16 ♗xd5 (16 ♕f6? ♖f8 17 ♕e6+ ♘e7∓) 16 ... ♕xf3 17 ♗xf3 0-0-0 18 d3 ♘d4 19 ♗e4 ½ : ½ Privorotsky – Selivanovsky, Mos-

cow 1963.

15 ... ♖f8

Interesting is **15 ... ♔d7!?** Tatai and Zinser suggest 16 ♕g7+ 16 ... ♔e6 17 ♕d1, but after 17 ... ♘d4 or 17 ... ♘e7, Black looks fine. Black can also cope with 16 ♕f7+, e.g. 16 ... ♔c8 17 ♗b3 ♕d4 18 ♕xd5 and now 18 ... ♖f8 or 18 ... ♘b4.

16 ♕e6+ ♔d8

Here, Nikitin gives the variation **16 ... ♗e7** 17 b4! ♕xb4 18 ♗xc6+ bxc6 19 ♕xc6+ ♔f7 20 ♕xd5+ ♔g7 21 d3! (not 21 ♕xe5+? because of 21 ... ♗f6 22 ♕xc7+ ♖f7 23 ♕c6 ♕b7!) 21 ... ♕d6 and White is a little better. Not however, 21 ... ♖ad8? 22 ♕xe5+ ♗f6 23 ♕xc7+ ♖f7 24 ♗h6+! ♔g8 25 ♖ab1±

17 b4

17 ♗b3 ♘d4 18 ♗xc4 ♘xe6 19 ♗xd5 ♘c5 20 b4 (20 d4 exd4 21 b4 ♘d3 22 ♗h6 ♖e8

23 ♗xb7 ♖b8∓ {Euwe}; 20
♖d1 c6∓) 20 ... ♘d3 21 ♗xb7
♖b8 22 ♗e4 ♘xc1 23 ♖fxc1
♖xb4 and Black obtained a
favourable ending, Lepe-
shkin – Bebchuk, Moscow
1963.

A critical position for the
variation

17 ...   ♕xb4

If 17 ... ♘xb4 then 18 d3
but more interesting is 17
... ♖e8!? with the possible
continuation 18 ♕f6+ (18
♕f7 ♕xb4) 18 ... ♗e7 19 ♕f7
♗xb4 20 ♕xh7 ♕d3 leading
to a very sharp position
where Black has counter-
play.

18   ♗xc6   bxc6
19   d4!   ♗e7

19 ... exd4 20 ♗h6! ♖e8 21
♗g5+ ♗e7 22 ♖ae1! ♖b8 (22
... ♕d6 23 ♗xe7+ ♕xe7 24
♕xc6+–) 23 ♕f7 d3 24 a3!
♕xa3 25 ♖xe7 ♖xe7 26 ♖e1
+–

20	♕xc6	♖b8
21	dxe5	♕d4
22	e6!	♔c8
23	♕d7+	♔b7
24	♖b1+	1 : 0

Bakhchevansky – Kayaski,
correspondence 1969. This
should serve as a warning
to Black not to let the position become too 'spaced
out'.

B2

10   ...   e4!

This energetic continua-
tion, associated with a
pawn sacrifice, creates
complex problems for
White.

11   ♕f5

11 ♘xf6+ ♕xf6 12 ♕xf6!
(12 ♕h5+ ♕f7 13 ♕xf7+ ♔xf7
14 f3 ♔g6!∓ Lein – Gheor-
ghiu, Sochi 1964) 12 ... gxf6
13 d3 0-0-0 14 dxe4 dxe4 15
♗e3 (Ligterink – Bohm, Wijk
aan Zee 1980) and now 15 ...

♘e5! leads to an unclear position.

11 ...   0-0!

11 ... ♕d7? 12 ♕xf6 gxf6 13 ♘xf6+ ♔e7 14 ♘xd7 ♔xd7 15 d3 left Black without compensation for the pawn, Nezhmetdinov – Bergin, Moscow 1963.

11 ... ♘xh5 12 ♕xh5+ g6 13 ♕h6 ♕f6 (13 ... ♕d7) 14 d3 0-0-0 15 ♗g5 ♕f5 16 dxe4 dxe4 17 ♗e3 h6 18 ♕xf5+ gxf5 19 ♖ad1 h5 (19 ... f4 20 ♗d4 ♖hg8 21 ♗c4) 20 ♗c4± Dvoiris – Smirin, Polanica Zdroj 1989.

Black is splendidly developed and is already threatening to launch an attack against the White king. Black's possibilities are illustrated by the game Zamanov – Agzamov, Youth Tournament 1965, which we now follow.

12 ♘xf6+   ♕xf6

13	♕xd5+	♔h8
14	♗xc6	bxc6
15	♕xe4	

15 ♕a5 ♕f4 16 g3 ♕h6 17 ♔g2 ♗xg3∓

15	...	♖ae8
16	♕c4	♖e1!
17	f4	♖xf1+
18	♕xf1	♗xf4
19	g3?	♗e3+
		0 : 1

It should be noted that after 19 ♕e2 ♕g5! 20 ♕g4 ♕e5! 21 ♕d1 ♕d4+ 22 ♔h1 ♗d6! White's cause is hopeless.

C

9   ♘h5

The most frequently seen continuation. White aims to exchange the enemy knight without wasting time castling.

9   ...   ♕d6!

With this move, Black safely overcomes the opening difficulties, but also worth consideration is the recommendation of *Schach - Archiv*, **9 ... e4 10** ♘xf6+ (10 ♕f5 ♔f7 11 ♘xf6 gxf6 12 ♕h5+ ♔g8! leads nowhere for White) **10 ...** ♕xf6 **11** ♕h5+ ♕f7 **12** ♕e5+ (Keres suggested 12 ♕xf7+ ♔xf7 13 ♗xc6 bxc6 14 f3 exf3 15 0-0 ♗c5+ 16 ♔h1, but after 16 ... ♖ae8! 17 ♖xf3+ ♔g6 18 ♖g3+ ♔h5! Black's advantage is clear) **12 ...** ♗e7 **13** ♗xc6+ bxc6 **14** ♕xc7 0-0 **15** 0-0 ♕e6⩱

On **9 ... a6** there can follow **10** ♗xc6+ bxc6 **11 0-0!**

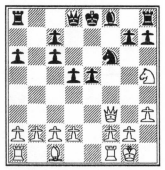

And now:

a) **11 ...** ♘d7 **12** d4 e4 **13** ♕g4! ♕e7 **14** ♗g5 ♕f7 **15** f3 g6 **16** ♘g3± Westerinen - Camilleri, Halle 1967.

b) **11 ...** ♕d6 **12** ♖e1 0-0-0 **13** ♕e2 ♘xh5 **14** ♕xh5 e4 **15** d3±

c) **11 ...** ♔f7 **12** d3 ♗d6 (12

... ♗e7 **13** g4; (12 ... g6 **13** ♘xf6 ♕xf6 **14** ♕g4 ♕e6 **15** ♕a4 ♗g7 **16** f4!↑) **13** ♗g5 ♖f8 **14** ♗xf6 gxf6 **15** ♘g3±

10 ♘xf6+ **gxf6**
11 ♕h5+ **♔d7**

Worth consideration is **11 ...** ♔e7 **12** c3 ♗g7 **13** ♗e2 (13 0-0 ♘d8 14 d4 ♘e6∞ Kristol - Ranniku, Moscow 1972) **13 ...** ♖af8 **14** ♗g4 e4 **15** d4 ♔d8 Olifer - Asaturian, Sochi 1965.

The strong pawn centre compensates adequately for the exposed position of Black's king.

12 ♕g4+
12 ♗e2 ♘d4

12 c3 ♖d8 (Kupreichik recommends 12 ... ♖e8 13 0-0 ♕e6 14 d4 ♗d6 15 ♗e3 ♖e7! with good play) **13** ♕g4+ ♕e6=

12 0-0 ♖d8 **13** d4 ♔c8 (13 ... exd4 is not as direct, e.g. 14 ♕g4+ ♕e6 15 ♕xd4 ♖g8

16 ♗f4 ♚c8 17 ♗xc6 ♛xc6 18 b4 ♛b6 19 ♛xb6 axb6= Bellin – Becx Guernsey 1990) 14 dxe5! (not 14 c3? ♛e6! 15 ♗xc6 bxc6 16 ♗e3 ♗d6 17 ♖ae1 ♖d7∓ Planinc – Parma, Ljubliana – Portoroz 1975) 14 ... fxe5 15 ♗g5 ♗e7 16 ♗xc6 bxc6 17 ♖ae1 ♗xg5 18 ♛xg5 ♖de8= Matulovic – Gasic, Birmingham 1975.

12	...	♛e6
13	♗xc6+	bxc6
14	♛xe6+	♚xe6

With the better chances for Black, Sergeyev – Glazkov, Moscow 1981.

9) 4 ♘c3 fxe4 5 ♘xe4 d5 6 ♘xe5

1	e4	e5
2	♘f3	♘c6
3	♗b5	f5
4	♘c3	fxe4
5	♘xe4	d5
6	♘xe5	

This popular continuation is accompanied by a temporary piece sacrifice which leads to a sharp and interesting struggle.

6	...	dxe4
7	♘xc6	

7 ♕h5+ g6 8 ♘xg6 hxg6 9 ♕xh8 is too risky as demonstrated by Solntsev - Selivanovsky, Moscow 1961 which continued 9 ... ♗e6!

10 ♕e5 ♔f7 11 ♕xe4 ♘f6 12 ♕e3 ♘b4 13 ♗a4 ♘bd5 14 ♕d4 ♗g7 15 d3 ♘d7 with excellent piece play.

A) 7 ... bxc6
B) 7 ... ♕d5

7 ... ♕g5 is examined in the next chapter.

A

7	...	bxc6

An interesting, but very risky choice.

8	♗xc6+	♗d7
9	♕h5+	♔e7
10	♕e5+	♗e6

11 ♗xa8!

The best. Others allow Black to escape the worst and organise counterplay:

a) **11 d4 ♔f7!** 12 ♗g5 (12 ♗xa8 ♕xa8 {12 ... ♗d6 13 ♕xe4 ♘f6 14 ♕f3 ♕xa8} 13 ♕xc7+ ♗e7 14 c4 ♘f6 15 d5 ♗d7 16 ♕f4 g5 17 ♕e3 ♗d6 18 ♗d2 ♖c8 and Black's active piece play gave him the advantage, Zuravlev - Starkov, Ulyanovsk 1960) 12 ... ♘f6 13 ♗xf6 (13 d5 ♗d7 14 ♗xa8 ♗d6!) 13 ... gxf6 14 ♕h5+ ♔g7 15 0-0-0 ♖b8 16 ♗xe4 ♕d7 17 ♖d3 ♗d6 18 ♕a5 ♖he8 and the two bishops gave Black the edge, Bannik - Mikenas, Vilnius 1957

b) **11 f4** and now Black can respond in two ways:

bi) **11 ... exf3** 12 d4 (if 12 0-0 ♖b8 13 d4 then 13 ... ♖b6 or 13 ... ♕d6 with sharp play) 12 ... ♘f6 13 d5 f2+! 14 ♔e2 ♘xd5 15 ♗g5+ ♘f6 16 ♖hd1 ♕c8 17 ♖d7+ ♕xd7! 18 ♗xd7 ♔xd7 19 ♕b5+ ♔e7 and Black has sufficient compensation for the queen, Kovalevsky - Lyubarsky, 1968.

bii) **11 ... ♘h6** 12 ♕xe4 ♖b8 13 d4 ♔f7 14 f5 ♗c4 15 b3 ♗b4+ 16 ♔d1 ♗c3 17 d5 ♕f6 18 ♕e6+ ♕xe6 19 fxe6+ ♔g6 20 bxc4 ♗xa1∓ Morozov - Starkov, Ulyanovsk 1960. Liberzon - A. Geller, Moscow - Leningrad (m) 1960 saw 12 f5 (instead of 12 ♕xe4) 12 ... ♘xf5 13 ♖f1. Black now blundered with 13 ... ♘d4?? and got mated after 14 ♕c5+! ♕d6 15 ♕g5+. However, with 13 ... ♕d6! 14 ♕xd6+ (on 14 ♕xe4 ♖b8 15 ♖xf5? there follows 15 ... ♖b4) 14 ... ♔xd6 15 ♗xa8 c6 Black could be looking for the advantage.

Finally, 13 0-0 (instead of 13 ♖f1 in the above variation) 13 ... ♕d4+ (better is 13 ... ♕d6!) 14 ♕xd4 ♘xd4 15 ♗xa8 ♘xc2 16 ♗xe4 ♘xa1 17 d4 ♔d7! 18 ♗f4 ♘b3 19 axb3 ♗d6 20 d5 ♗g4 21 h3 ♗xf4 22 ♖xf4 ♗h5 23 g4 ♗g6 ½ : ½ was Shavernayev - Starkov, Ulyanovsk 1960.

11   ...   ♕xa8

12 ♕xc7+ ♔e8

12 ... ♔f6 13 0-0! ♔g6 (13 ... ♗e7 14 f3! and 13 ... ♕d5 14 b3 ♗e7 15 ♗b2+ ♔f7 16 d3! don't help Black) 14 d3 ♘f6 15 ♖e1 h5 16 ♕g3+ ♔h7 17 dxe4± Smejkal - Duckstein, 1969.

12 ... ♗d7 13 d3 ♘f6 14 0-0 h6 15 dxe4 ♘e8 16 ♕a5 ♗e6 17 ♗e3 a6 18 ♖ae1 ♔f7 19 ♕a4 ♗e7 20 f4+- Adamski - Nilsson, Skopje 1962.

13 0-0 ♗e7
14 d3

White has a rook and two pawns for two minor pieces, and the exposed position of the black king gives him every hope for victory. Practical examples are:

a) **14 ... ♘f6** 15 ♗g5! ♔f7 16 dxe4 ♖c8 (16 ... ♕xe4 17 ♖ae1) 17 ♕f4 ♖xc2 18 ♖ac1! Hennings - Lanka, Riga 1971.

b) **14 ... ♔f7** 15 ♗e3 ♘f6 16 dxe4 ♖c8 17 ♕xa7 ♕xe4 18

c3 ♘d5 19 ♖fe1 ♕g6 20 ♔h1 Evans - Duckstein, Lugano 1968.

c) **14 ... exd3** 15 cxd3 ♕d5. This (recommended by B. Nesterenko) is probably Black's best try, but White still stands well.

B

7 ... ♕d5

This variation first appeared in practice in 1950 and has successfully survived the test of time over 40 years.

8 c4

8 ♘xa7+ c6 9 c4 ♕c5! and White loses a piece.

8 ... ♕d6!

The old move was 8 ... ♕g5? which is disastrous following 9 d4 ♕xg2 10 ♕h5+. The text move breathes life into the variation and was first used by Candidate Master Agrinsky against Krogius in Moscow 1950.

We now examine the following possibilities:

B1) 9 c5
B2) 9 ♕h5
B3) 9 ♘xa7+

B1)

9 c5 ♕xc5

10 ♕a4

10 ... ♘f6

10 ... ♗d7 is unsatisfactory. Beggi – Contendini, Rome 1962 continued 11 ♕xe4+ ♘e7 12 ♘xe7 ♗xb5 13 ♘g6+ ♔d7 14 ♘e5+ ♔c8 and after 15 a4! Black didn't have a decent reply as 15 ... ♗xa4? 16 ♖xa4! ♕xc1+ 17 ♔e2 ♕xh1 18 ♕f5+ leads to mate and 15 ... ♗e8 16 b4! ♕xb4 17 ♕f5+ ♔b8 18 0-0! gives White a decisive attack.

11 d4

Tempting but mistaken is **11 ♘e5+?** c6 12 ♘xc6 bxc6 13 ♗xc6+ ♗d7 14 ♗xd7+ ♘xd7 15 ♕xe4+ because of the prosaic answer 15 ... ♕e5 and Black must win.

11 ... exd3

Others are also possible:

a) **11 ... ♕d6** 12 ♗f4!? ♕xf4 13 ♘e5+ c6! 14 ♗xc6+ bxc6 15 ♕xc6+ ♘d7!∞ (Gipslis).

b) **11 ... ♕b6** 12 ♘e5+ c6 13 ♗c4 ♗b4+∓ Rantanen – Sollid, Gausdal 1981. An example of further play from here is Hunerkopf – Seyffer, Bundesliga 1989 – 14 ♔f1 ♖f8 15 ♗e3 ♘g4 16 ♘xg4 ♗xg4 17 ♕b3 0-0-0 18 ♗e6+ ♗xe6 19 ♕xe6+ ♔b8 20 ♕xe4 ♕b5+ 21 ♔g1 ♗d6 22 ♕c2 ♗f4 23 h4 h6 24 ♖h3 g5 25 hxg5 hxg5 26 ♖f3 ♖h8 27 ♗xf4+ gxf4 28 ♕d2 ♔a8 29 ♖e1 ♖dg8 30 ♖e5 ♕c4 31 ♖e1 ♕d5 32 ♕xf4 ♕h5 33 ♔f1 ♕b5+ 34 ♔g1 ♕h5 35 ♔f1 ♕b5+ 36 ♔g1 ♕h5 37 ♔f1 ½-½

12 0-0

12 ♗e3 can be met by 12 ... d2+ or 12 ... ♕d6 13 0-0-0 bxc6! with the advantage for Black in both cases.

12 ... ♗d6!

12 ... bxc6? 13 ♗xc6+ ♗d7 14 ♗xd7+ ♔d8 15 ♗c6 and White went on to win,

Sukhanov - Shcharansky, Moscow 1967.

13 ♘e5+

13 ♖e1+ ♔f8 14 ♗e3 ♕h5.

13 ... c6
14 ♘xc6 0-0!

Black's chances are preferable, (S. Sinitsin).

B2

9 ♕h5+ g6
10 ♕e5+

10 ♘e5+ c6 11 ♘xg6 ♕xg6 12 ♕e5+ ♘e7 (12 ... ♔f7 13 ♕xh8 ♗g7) 13 ♕xh8 ♕xg2 is totally unacceptable for White.

10 ... ♕xe5
11 ♘xe5+ c6
12 ♗a4

12 ♘xc6? a6 13 ♘d4+ (13 ♗a4 ♗d7) 13 ... axb5 14 ♘xb5 ♔d8 and White has insufficient compensation for the missing piece.

12 ... ♗g7

Alternatively:

a) 12 ... ♗d6 13 d4 exd3 14 ♗f4 ♘f6 15 0-0-0 0-0 16 ♘xg6 d2+ 17 ♖xd2 ♗xf4 18 ♘xf4 ♘e4 19 ♖d4 ♖xf4 20 ♗c2 ♗f5 Maizhanov - Bogomolov, Moscow 1964, and following further interesting complications, the game ended as a draw.

b) 12 ... ♗e6 13 b3 (13 d4 exd3 14 0-0 or 14 ♗d2 △

0-0-0 are both approximately equal.) 13 ... ♗g7 14 ♗b2 a6 15 b4 (15 c5 ♘e7) 15 ... ♘h6 16 0-0 0-0 17 ♗b3 a5 18 bxa5 ♖xa5 19 d4 exd3 20 ♘xd3 ♗xb2 21 ♘xb2 ♖d8 with good compensation for the pawn, Velimiriovic - Vasyukov, Yugoslavia - USSR 1973.

13 d4

13 f4 exf3 14 ♘xf3 ♗f5 (more reliable is 14 ... ♗g4! as in Novopashin - Nikitin, Yalta 1962 where there followed 15 0-0 0-0-0 16 ♗c2 ♘e7 17 ♗e4 ♘f5 18 h3 ♘g3 19 hxg4 ♘xe4 20 ♖b1 ♘c5∓) 15 d4 0-0-0 16 ♗f4 ♗d3 17 ♗b3 with good play for White, as after 17 ... ♗xd4? 18 0-0-0 follows.

13 ... exd3
14 ♗f4

14 ♘xd3 is met by 14 ... ♗f5 and Black develops considerable activity. Lach-

ut - Mohring, 1958 continued 15 ♘c5 15 ... 0-0-0 16 0-0 ♘f6 17 ♖e1 ♘d7 18 ♘xd7 ♖xd7 19 ♗e3 ♗xb2 20 ♖ad1 ♖hd8 21 ♖xd7 ♖xd7 and following the rash capture 22 ♗xa7? Black responded with the advance 22 ... b5! and White realised that he had lost a piece. Passerotti - Tatai, Rome 1979 saw instead the more sensible 15 ♘f4 0-0-0 16 0-0 ♘f6 17 ♗e3 ♘g4 and the Black position is slightly, but nevertheless clearly, better.

14 0-0 is also worthy of consideration. After 14 ... ♗xe5? 15 ♖e1 ♗e6 16 ♖xe5 ♔f7 17 ♗b3 ♘f6 18 ♗g5 White gets the advantage, so a preferable alternative is 14 ... ♗f5 (14 ... ♗e6!? is an alternative which can be considered worthy of consideration, one example of this continuation is 15 ♗f4 0-0-0 16 ♖ad1 ♖d4 17 ♗g3 ♘f6 18 ♖fe1 d2 19 ♖e2 ♘e4 20 ♘f3 ♗g4 21 ♘xd4 ♘xg3 22 ♖exd2 ♗xd1 23 ♗xd1 ♖d8 24 ♗g4+ ♘f5 25 ♘xf5 ♖xd2 26 ♘xg7+ ♔b8 27 b3 ♖xa2∞ Madl - Elstner, Balatonbereny 1988) 15 ♖e1 0-0-0! leading to the following position:

Now White has two ways to play:

a) **16 ♘f7** d2 17 ♗xd2 ♖xd2 18 ♖e8+ ♔d7 19 ♖ae1 ♗d4 20 ♘xh8 (20 ♔h1 ♗xf2 21 ♖1e2 ♖xe2 22 ♖xe2 ♘h4 23 ♘xh8 ♘h6∓) 20 ... ♗xf2+ 21 ♔h1 ♗xe1 22 ♖xe1 ♖xb2∓

b) **16 ♗g5** d2 17 ♖e2 ♖e8 18 f4 (18 ♗f4 g5 19 ♗g3 h5! or 19 ... ♘h6) 18 ... h6 19 ♗h4 g5 20 ♗g3 ♗d3 21 ♖xd2 ♗xe5 22 fxe5 (22 ♖xd3 gxf4 23 ♗h4 ♗xb2∓) 22 ... ♗xc4=

Better than 17 ♖e2 looks 17 ♖e3!? ♖f8 but even then Black retains good chances, e.g. 18 f4 (18 ♖d1 h6 19 ♗h4 g5 20 ♗g3 h5) 18 ... ♘f6 19 ♗xf6 ♗xf6 20 ♖d1 ♖d8.

14 ...   ♘f6

14 ... ♗e6 15 0-0-0 0-0-0 16 ♖he1 ♖d4 17 ♗d2 ♗xc4 18 ♗c3 d2+ 19 ♖xd2 ♖xd2 20 ♔xd2 ♗d5 21 ♘g4!= Volchok - Olifer, 1961.

14 ... g5?! 15 ♗g3 ♗f5 16

0-0!↑ Rodriguez - Barreras, Cienfuegos 1979.

15	♘xd3	♗f5
16	0-0-0	0-0-0
17	♗c2	♖d4

18 ♗e5

18 ♗e3 ♖xc4 19 b3 ♖xc2+! 20 ♔xc2 ♖d8 21 f3 ♘d5 22 ♗d2 g5 23 ♖he1 c5 24 ♖e4 ♖d6 25 ♖de1 h6 26 ♘f2 ♗d4 27 ♘d3 ♘f6∓ Spasov - Mohring, Zinnowitz 1965.

18	...	♖xc4
19	♗c3	♖xc3!
20	bxc3	♘e4
21	♖de1	♘xc3
22	a4	♖d8
23	♘c5	♗h6+
24	♔b2	♖d2

and White soon resigned, Kristiansen - Mohring, Tel Aviv 1964.

B3

9 ♘xa7+

This continuation is certainly the strongest!

9	... ♗d7

Others are clearly in White's favour:

a) 9 ... ♔d8 10 ♘xc8 ♔xc8 11 d4 exd3 12 0-0

b) 9 ... c6 10 ♘xc8 ♖xc8 11 ♗a4 ♘f6 12 0-0 ♗e7 13 d4! exd3 14 c5! and now:

bi) 14 ... ♕d7 15 ♗b3 ♖d8 16 ♗g5 ♕d4 17 ♖e1 ♖f8 18 ♕h5+ ♔d7 19 ♕h3+± Thiemann - Harbers, Correspondence 1982.

bii) 14 ... ♕xc5 15 ♕xd3 0-0 16 ♗e3 ♕h5 17 ♘d1 ♕h4 18 ♗f3 ♔h8 19 ♕d4! Thiemann - Harbers, Correspondence 1982.

10	♗xd7+	♕xd7

Now White's two choices are:

B31) 11 ♘b5
B32) 11 ♕h5+

B31

11	♘b5	♘f6

12   0-0

12   ...   ♗c5

The text continuation was worked out by Asaturyan. In the event of **12 ... c6** 13 ♘c3 ♗c5 (better 13 ... ♗e7) 14 d4 exd3 White has the strong 15 ♗e3! (In Cullip - Becx, Guernsey 1988 White played the inferior 15 ♖e1+ and Black obtained sufficient counterplay for the sacrificed pawn. The game resulted in an instructive draw - 15 ... ♔f7 16 ♗e3 ♗xe3 17 ♖xe3 ♖ad8 18 ♕f3 ♖he8 19 ♘e4 ♕d4 20 ♘xf6 ♖xe3 21 fxe3 ♕xf6 22 ♖d1 ♔e7 23 ♖d2 ♕e5 24 ♕f4 ♔e6 25 ♔f2 ♖d7 26 ♔e1 ♕xf4 27 exf4 ♔f5 28 ♖f2 ♖d4 29 ♔d2 ♖xc4 30 ♔xd3 ♖xf4 31 ♖xf4+ ♔xf4 32 ♔d4 b6 33 a4 ♔f5 34 b4 ♔e6 35 ♔c4 ♔d6 36 a5 ♔c7 37 h4 ♔b7 38 h5 ♔a7 39 axb6+ ♔xb6 40 g4 ½-½) when

Gligoric - Heidenfeld, Madrid 1960 went 15 ... ♗xe3 16 fxe3 0-0 17 ♖f4 ♖ad8 18 ♕f3 ♕e6 19 ♘e4 ♘xe4 20 ♕xe4±

Also of interest is **12 ... ♗e7!?** 13 d4 exd3 14 ♗e3 c6 15 ♘c3 0-0

when the following are possible:

a) **16 f3** ♗d6! 17 ♔h1 ♖ad8

b) **16 ♘a4** ♕f5! 17 ♕b3 ♘g4! Prins - Trapl, Correspondence 1960.

c) **16 ♕d2** ♘g4 17 ♘d1 ♕d6 18 f4 ♘xe3 19 ♕xe3 ♗f6 20 ♔h1 ♖ae8 21 c5 ♕d5 Santa - Mohring, Correspondence 1961.

In all cases, Black has good chances.

13   d4

13 b4!? ♗xb4? 14 ♖b1 ♗c5 15 d4 exd3 16 ♖b3 0-0 17 ♖xd3± Sznapik - Polaizer, Ljubljana 1981. Black had to try 13 ... ♗d4 14 ♘xd4

♕xd4 15 ♖b1 ♕xc4∞

13   **...**   **exd3**

14   **♖e1+**

If **14 ♗f4** Black has time to reply 14 ... 0-0, as 15 ♗xc7? ♘e4 16 ♗g3 ♘xg3 17 hxg3 ♖xf2! 18 ♖xf2 ♖f8 is unacceptable for White.

14   **...**   **♔f7**

15   **♗e3**

15 ♗f4 ♖he8 16 ♖e3!? (16 ♘xc7? ♖xe1+ 17 ♕xe1 ♘g4 18 ♗g3 ♗xf2+! Haag – Hennings, 1965) 16 ... ♖xe3! (16 ... ♗xe3 17 fxe3) 17 fxe3 ♖e8 18 ♕f3 c6 19 ♘c3 ♕f5 20 ♘a4 g5!∓

15   **...**   **♗xe3**

16   **♖xe3**   **♖ad8**

In spite of the pawn deficit Black's chances are not worse here as the following games confirm.

a) 17 ♕f3 ♖he8 18 ♖d1 c6 19 ♘c3 ♕d4 20 ♖xe8 (20 h3 ♖xe3 21 ♕xe3 ♕xc4) 20 ... ♖xe8 21 h3 d2!= Kosenkov

– Asaturyan, Moscow 1962.

b) 17 ♕d2 ♖he8 18 ♖ae1 (18 ♖d1 ♖xe3! 19 fxe3 {19 ♕xe3? ♕g4!} 19 ... ♘e4∓) 18 ... ♖xe3 19 ♖xe3 c6 20 ♘c3 ♕d4 21 b3 ♕xc3!! 22 ♕xc3 d2-+ Maresov – Shekhtman, Ioshkar – Ola 1964.

c) 17 ♕b3 ♖he8 18 ♖d1 (18 c5+ ♔f8 19 ♖d1 d2) 18 ... c5 19 ♘c3 ♖xe3 20 fxe3 ♕e7 21 ♘d5 ♖xd5! 22 cxd5 ♕xe3+ 23 ♔h1 ♘e4! 24 d6+ ♔f6! 25 ♖f1+ ♔e5 26 ♕f7 ♔xd6-+ (Estrin)

B32

11   **♕h5+**   **g6**

11 ... ♔d8 12 ♕a5 ♔e8 13 0-0! ♘f6 14 d4! exd3 15 ♗e3±

12   **♕e5+**   **♔f7**

13   **♘b5**

It is dangerous for White to take the rook, e.g. **13 ♕xh8** ♘f6 14 ♘b5 c6! 15 ♘c3 ♖e8 (Trapl's 15 ... ♕g4!) 16

b3 (16 0-0 ♕d3! 17 ♖e1 ♗c5
18 ♕xe8+ ♔xe8 19 ♘d1 ♘g4
20 ♘e3 ♘xe3 21 fxe3 ♗b4 22
♖f1 ♕xc4∓) 16 ... ♗c5 17
♕xe8+ ♔xe8 18 h3 (18 0-0
♕d3 {also good is 18 ...
♘g4! 19 ♘d1 ♕d6 20 g3 ♕e5
21 ♗b2 ♕h5 22 h4 g5} 19 ♗b2
♕xd2 20 ♘a4 ♗d4 21 ♖ad1
♗xf2+ 22 ♔h1 ♕f4 23 ♗xf6
♕xf6 24 ♖de1 ♕h4!-+ Heil-
emann – Florian, Corres-
pondence 1975/76) 18 ...
♕d3 19 ♖f1 ♘h5 20 g3 ♗d4
21 ♗a3 ♗xc3! 22 dxc3 ♕xc3+
23 ♔e2 ♕c2+ 24 ♔e1 e3! 25
fxe3 ♘xg3-+ Ruban – Med-
ler, Minsk 1964.

13 ... c6

14 ♕d4

a) **14 ♘c3 ♖e8!** 15 ♕a5 (15
♕xh8 ♘f6) 15 ... ♘f6 16 h3
♗d6 17 c5 ♖e5 (17 ... ♕f5) 18
b4 ♗c7 19 ♕a4 ♖d8 20 ♕b3+
♔g7 21 0-0 ♕f5!∓

b) **14 b3 ♘f6** (14 ... ♖e8)
15 ♗b2 ♗g7 16 ♘c3 ♘g4 with

a very active position for
Black, Malmberg – Strom-
berg, Correspondence 1964.

14 ... ♕e7

Others:

a) **14 ... ♘f6** 15 ♕xd7+
♘xd7 16 ♘c3 ♘c5 17 0-0
♗g7 18 f3±

b) **14 ... ♕g4** 15 0-0! cxb5
(15 ... ♗g7 16 ♘d6+) 16 f3
♕h4 (16 ... ♕e6 17 fxe4+ ♘f6
18 e5; 16 ... ♕h5 also failed
to help Black in Jacobs –
Garcia, Benidorm 1989, e.g.
17 fxe4+ ♔e6 18 b4! {not 18
♕xh8? ♗d6! intending 19 ...
♗e5. Meanwhile Black was
threatening 18 ... ♗c5} 18 ...
♗xb4 19 e5! ♖f8 {19 ... ♕xe5
20 ♕xe5+ and 21 ♗b2+} 20
♖xf8 ♗xf8 21 ♕d5+ ♔e7 22
♗a3+ ♔e8 23 ♕xb5+ ♔d8 24
♗xf8 1-0) 17 ♕d5+! ♔e8 18
♕xb5+ ♔d8 19 fxe4 ♗d6 20
e5 ♕d4+ 21 ♔h1±

c) **14 ... ♕f5** 15 ♘d6+ (15
♕xh8) 15 ... ♗xd6 16 ♕xd6
♘e7 17 0-0 ♖hd8 18 ♕b4
♖d3 19 ♕xb7 ♖ad8 20 b3
and White slowly realised
his advantage in the game
Ciocaltea – Malich, Sinaia
1964.

d) **14 ... ♕xd4** 15 ♘xd4
♗g7 16 ♘e2 ♖a4 17 b3! and
Black has insufficient compensation for the pawn
sacrifice, e.g. 17 ... ♗xa1 (17

... ♖xc4 18 bxc4 ♗xa1 19 0-0
♘f6 20 ♗a3 ♖a8 {20 ... ♕e5
21 ♖b1} 21 ♖xa1 ♖xa3 22 ♘c3
Jansa - Vera, Bratislava
1983) 18 bxa4 ♘f6 19 0-0
♖a8 20 ♗a3! ♖xa4 (20 ...
♕e5 21 ♖b1!) 21 ♖xa1 ♖xa3 22
♘c3 (Despotovic). Know-
ledge of this analysis
proved fruitful in Frolik -
Seyffer, Bundesliga 1988,
when White went on to win
after 22 ♘c3 ♔e6 23 ♖b1
♖a7 24 ♔f1 ♔e5 25 ♔e2 ♔d4
26 ♖b4 ♔c5 27 a3 ♔d4 28 h3
h5 29 c5+ ♔xc5 30 ♘xe4+
♘xe4 31 ♖xe4 ♖xa3 32 ♖e6
b5 33 ♖xg6 b4 34 ♖g5+ ♔c4
35 ♖xh5 b3 36 ♖h4+ ♔c5 37
♔d3 b2+ 38 ♔c2 ♖b3 39 ♔b1
♔d5 40 ♖f4 c5 41 h4 c4 42
h5 ♔c5 43 h6 ♖b4 44 g3 c3
45 dxc3 1-0

e) **14 ... ♖d8** 15 ♕xd7+
♖xd7 16 ♘c3 ♘f6

Here, in spite of the two
extra pawns, White is ess-

entially unable to strengthen his position, e.g.

a) **17 b3** ♗c5 18 ♘a4 ♗a7
19 ♗b2 ♖hd8= Vogt - Moh-
ring, Leipzig 1975.

b) **17 0-0** ♗c5 18 ♖b1 ♖a8
19 b3 ♔e6 20 ♖e1 ♔f5 21 ♖b2
g5 22 ♖c2 ♖ad8 23 ♖e2 h5
24 ♗b2 g4 25 ♘d1 ♘h7 and
Black's chances are not
worse, Augustin - Mohring,
Stary Smokovec 1976.

c) **17 ♖f1** ♗c5 18 f3 exf3 19
♖xf3 ♔g7 20 b3 ♘g4 21 ♗b2
♖e8+ 22 ♔d1 ♔g8 23 ♔c2
♘xh2 24 ♖g3 ♗f2 25 ♖d3
♖f7 26 a4 ♗c5= and Black
held the balance in Ivanov -
Rocha, Mexico 1980.

15 ♘c3

After 15 ♕xh8 there can
follow 15 ... ♘f6 16 b3 ♖d8
(16 ... cxb5? 17 ♗b2! or 16 ...
♖e8 17 ♗b2 ♔g7 18 ♘a3 c5 19
♕xe8+ ♘xe8 20 ♖d1 ♗e5 21
d4 exd3 22 0-0 ♘f6 23 ♖xd3
♗xh2+ 24 ♔xh2 ♕e2 25 ♖f3

♛xf1 26 ♗b2 ♛e2 27 ♗xf6
♔g8 28 ♘c3 ♛c2 29 ♘d5 h5
30 ♗c3 ♛xa2 31 ♘e7+ ♔h7
32 ♖f7+ ♔h6 33 ♘g8+ ♔g5
34 f4+ 1-0 Watson – Cooper,
Saint John 1988) 17 ♗b2 ♗g7
18 ♛xd8 ♛xd8 19 ♘a3 (on 19
♘d4 there follows 19 ... c5
20 ♘b5 ♛d3∓ but deserving
of attention is 19 ♘c3 ♘g4
20 0-0-0) and now Black
can obtain the advantage
with the elegant 19 ... ♘g4
20 0-0-0 ♘xf2! 21 ♖hf1
♗xb2+ 22 ♔xb2 ♔g7.

White can attempt to
strengthen the above var-
iation with 18 ♗a3 ♛d7 19
♘d6+ ♔e6 20 ♛xd8 (not 20
♘xb7?? ♛xd2+) 20 ... ♛xd8
21 ♘xb7. The correspond-
ence game Buresh – Sheshil,
1980/81 continued 21 ...
♛d4? 22 0-0 ♘g4 23 ♖ae1
1 : 0. Lawton – Finlayson,
England 1985 saw instead 21
... ♛b6? 22 ♘c5+ ♔f7 23 0-0
♛a5 24 ♘a4±. In our opin-
ion the correct path is 21 ...
♛c7! 22 ♘c5+ ♔f7 and a
satisfactory continuation
for White is not clear, e.g.
23 0-0 ♘g4! It may be that
23 ♗b2, challenging on the
long diagonal, is White's
best. However, the position
remains highly complex,
e.g. 23 ♗b2 h5!? 24 h3 e3 25

0-0 (not 25 dxe3? ♛a5+) 25
... e2 26 ♖fe1 ♘g4!? 27 hxg4
♗xb2 28 ♖ab1 ♗d4 29 ♘e4
hxg4 30 g3 ♛a5 31 a4 ♔g7
32 ♖xe2 ♛f5 33 ♖be1 ♛f3 34
♖e3 ♗xe3 35 ♖xe3± and the
coordinated White forces
proved to be the more ef-
ficient and he went on to
win in Jacobs – Julian, Benidorm 1989.

15 ... ♘f6
16 ♛e3

16 0-0 ♖d8 17 ♛e3 ♖d3 18
♛e2 ♛e5 19 ♖e1 (19 f4 ♛d4+
20 ♔h1 {Santo – Mallée,
Correspondence 1980} 20 ...
♗b4! 21 b3 ♖d8 and Black
has very strong pressure)
19 ... ♗d6 20 g3 ♖e8 21 ♛xd3
exd3 22 ♖xe5 ♗xe5 23 ♔f1
(23 ♘d1 ♗d4 24 ♘e3 ♘e4∓
Rudak – Klompus, Corres-
pondence 1972) 23 ... ♗d4 24
f3 g5 25 g4 h5 26 h3 ♔g6 27
♖b1 hxg4 28 hxg4 ♘d7 with
sufficient compensation
for the two pawns, as in
the correspondence game,
Petrushka – Wittman, played in 1978.

16 ... ♖d8
17 d4 exd3
18 ♛xe7+ ♗xe7

In order to ease the
defensive task, White is
obligated to return one
pawn.

Black has enough compensation for the pawn.

19   ♗d2

19 ♗e3 ♗b4 20 0-0-0 ♗xc3 21 bxc3 ♘e4 22 ♗d4 ♖he8 23 ♖xd3 (Kostro - Witkowski, 1966) and now Black should continue 23 ... c5! 24 ♖f3+ ♔g8 25 ♗e3 (25 ♗f6 ♖a8!) 25 ... ♖d3 26 ♔b2 ♘xf2! 27 ♗xf2 ♖xf3 28 gxf3 ♖e2+=

	19	...	♖d4
	20	b3	♘e4
	21	♘xe4	♖xe4+
	22	♗e3	♗b4+
	23	♔f1	b5
	24	cxb5	cxb5
	25	g3	♖c8=

Sorokin - Kaminnik, USSR 1966.

10) 4 ♘c3 fxe4 5 ♘xe4 d5
6 ♘xe5 dxe4 7 ♘xc6 ♕g5

1	e4	e5
2	♘f3	♘c6
3	♗b5	f5
4	♘c3	fxe4
5	♘xe4	d5
6	♘xe5	dxe4
7	♘xc6	♕g5

This heavily analysed continuation leads to a complex struggle. Although this continuation has, of course, been known and researched for many years, it was given a new lease of life by Speelman's adoption of it for a critical game from his World Championship Semi-Final match against Jan Timman. The result was a crushing victory for Black which helped to keep alive Speelman's chances in the match.

This high level exposure was also a tremendous advertisement for the Schliemann in general, which has thus been thrust into the forefront of theoretical research. The main adherents of this variation for Black are the grandmasters Inkiov and Klinger, who have both used it to score well against high class opposition.

8 ♕e2

8 c4 ♘f6 9 ♘xa7+ c6 10 ♘xc6 bxc6 11 ♗xc6+ ♔f7 12 ♗xa8 ♕xg2 13 ♖f1 ♗h3 14 ♕e2 ♗c5 15 ♗d5+ ♘xd5 16 cxd5 ♖e8 17 a4 ♗g4-+ Mazzoni - Boey, Correspondence 1966.

8   ...   ♘f6

8 ... ♕xg2? is a gross error on account of 9 ♕h5+

8 ... ♗d7 is poor after 9 ♕xe4+ ♘e7 10 ♘xe7 ♗xb5 (10 ... ♕xb5 11 ♘g6+ ♔f7 12 ♘xh8+ ♔g8 13 a4! ♕a6 14 ♕d5+ ♗e6 15 ♕b5±) 11 ♘g6+ ♔d7 12 d3! ♕xg6 13 ♕d5+±

9   f4

9 ♘xa7+ ♗d7! 10 ♗xd7+ ♘xd7! gives Black excellent chances. Thomas - Bosh-kovich, USA 1975 continued 11 ♕xe4+ (11 ♘b5 ♕xg2 12 ♖f1 0-0-0 with a very strong attack) 11 ... ♔d8! 12 ♕xb7 (12 d3 ♕a5+) 12 ... ♖xa7! 13 ♕xa7 ♕xg2 14 ♖f1 ♗c5∓

After 9 f4 Black has two separate paths:

A) 9 ... ♕xf4
B) 9 ... ♕h4+

A

9   ...   ♕xf4

And now:

A1) 10 ♘xa7+
A2) 10 d4
A3) 10 ♘e5+

A1

10   ♘xa7+

L. Svenonius proposed this move as a refutation of 9 ... ♕xf4.

10   ...   ♗d7

10 ... c6 11 ♘xc8

10 ... ♔d8 11 ♘xc8 ♔xc8 is bad after 12 d4, e.g 12 ... ♕h4+ (12 ... ♕f5 13 ♗c4 ♗d6 14 ♖f1 ♕a5+ 15 ♗d2 ♕b6 16 0-0-0!± Suchko - Myasni-kov, Kishinev 1962) 13 g3 ♕h3 14 ♗f4 ♘d5 15 ♕xe4!± Gufeld - Myasnikov, Riga 1960.

11   ♗xd7+   ♔xd7

11 ... ♘xd7 12 ♘b5 0-0-0 13 d4 and Black has in-sufficient for the pawn, e.g. 13 ... ♕f6 (13 ... ♕f7 14 ♖f1 ♕d5 15 c4 ♗b4+ 16 ♔f2) 14 ♕c4! c6 15 ♖f1

12   d4

Others:

a) 12 ♘b5 ♖e8 (12 ... c6 13 ♘c3 ♗d6) 13 b3 ♗b4 14 c3 ♗c5 15 ♗a3 ♕e5 16 ♗xc5 ♕xc5 17 b4 ♕e5 18 0-0 h5 19 ♘d4 ♔c8 20 ♖f5 ♕d6 21

♘b5 ♕b6+=

b) **12 ♕b5+ ♔e6 13 ♕c4+ ♔d7** (13 ... ♘d5 14 ♘b5 ♗d6 15 ♘d4+ ♔e5 16 ♖f1 and Black has to surrender the queen) **14 ♘b5** (14 ♕b5+ ♔e6=) 14 ... c6 (14 ... ♗d6) 15 ♕d4+ ♔c8 16 g3 ♕f5 17 ♘d6+ ♗xd6 18 ♕xd6 ♖e8 19 ♕f4 ♕xf4 20 gxf4 ♘d5∓

12	...	♕h4+
13	g3	♕h3

Black's positional advantages compensate for the missing pawn.

14 ♘b5

14 ♕b5+ ♔e6 15 ♕e5+ ♔d7 (15 ... ♔f7!? 16 ♕xc7+ ♔g6 17 ♕xb7 ♗d6) 16 ♕b5+ (16 ♘b5 c6 17 ♘c3 ♗d6) leads to repetition.

14	...	c6
15	♘c3	♗b4!
16	♗f4	♘d5
17	♔d2	

17 0-0-0? ♗xc3 18 bxc3 ♘xf4! 19 gxf4 ♕xc3 and

Black won easily, Orlovsky - Lipsky, Warsaw 1976.

17	...	e3+!
18	♔c1	♗xc3
19	bxc3	b5

Belchuk - Lipsky, Warsaw 1975. Black has excellent chances.

A2

10	d4

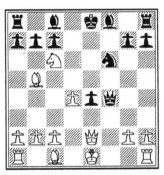

10	...	♕d6!

10 ... ♕f5 is bad after 11 ♖f1! as is 10 ... ♕h4+ 11 g3 ♕h3 12 ♗g5! - see game no. 7, Fischer - Matulovic.

11 ♘e5+

A faulty path for White is **11 ♘xa7+?** which comes unstuck as demonstrated in two recent games: 11 ... c6 12 ♘xc8 ♕b4+! 13 c3 ♕xb5 14 ♕xb5 cxb5 15 a4 (15 ♘b6 ♖a6 traps the knight) 15 ... ♖xc8 (15 ... bxa4? 16 ♘b6 would be a mistake) 16 axb5 ♗d6 17 ♖a7 (Remarkably this entire sequence was repeated in Brinck - Claussen - Welling, Lyngby open 1989. White now deviated with 17 0-0 but it didn't alter the outcome - 17 ... 0-0 18 ♗f4 ♘e8 19 ♗e3 ♗b8 20 ♖xf8+ ♔xf8 21 ♖f1+ ♔g8 22 ♖f5 ♘d6 23 ♖e5 ♔f7 24 ♔f2 ♘c4 25 ♖xe4 ♘xb2 26 ♗g5 ♘d1+ 27 ♔e1 ♘xc3 28 ♖e7+ ♔g6 29 h4 ♘xb5 30 d5 ♘d6 31 ♗f4 ♘f5 32 ♖e6+ ♔f7 33 ♗xb8 ♖xb8 34 h5 ♖e8 0-1) 17 ... 0-0! 18 ♖xb7 ♘g4 19 ♖f1 (19 h3 ♘f2 20 ♖g1 ♗h2 21 ♖f1 ♘d3+ 22 ♔e2 ♖xf1 23 ♔xf1 ♘xc1-+) 19 ... ♗xh2 20 ♖xf8+ ♖xf8 21 ♖e7 ♖f2!-+ (21 ... ♗g3+ 22 ♔e2 ♖f2+ 23 ♔d1 ♖xg2 24 b6 h5 25 b7) 22 ♖xe4 ♖xg2 23 ♗d2 ♗g3+ 24 ♔f1 ♖f2+ 25 ♔g1 ♘h2! 0-1 Georgiev Kir - Inkiov, Bulgaria 1988. Notes based on Inkiov's in *Informator*.

11 ... c6

12 ♗c4 ♗e6

12 ... ♕xd4 is doubtful after 13 ♗f4 (not 13 ♘f7? ♗g4) 13 ... ♘d5 (13 ... ♗c5 14 c3!) 14 ♖d1 ♗b4+ (or 14 ... ♘xf4 15 ♖xd4 ♘xe2 16 ♖xe4 ♗b4+ 17 ♔xe2) 15 c3 ♘xf4 16 ♖xd4 ♘xe2 17 ♔xe2 ♗c5 18 ♖xe4 ♗f5 19 ♖f4±

13 ♗f4

The immediate **13 c3!** deserves attention, e.g. 13 ... ♗e7 14 0-0 0-0 15 ♗f4 ♗xc4 16 ♘xc4! ♕e6 and White preserves the better chances.

13 ... ♗xc4

13 ... 0-0-0 14 c3 ♗xc4 15 ♕xc4 ♘d5 also looks perfectly okay for Black. Hernandez - Alzate, Cali Zonal 1990.

14 ♕xc4 ♕d5

15 ♕b3 ♗d6!?

15 ... ♕xb3 16 axb3 ♘d5! 17 0-0 ♗d6! 18 ♗g3 (worse is 18 ♖ae1 0-0 19 ♖xe4 c5! 20 c3 cxd4 21 cxd4 ♖ac8 with good counterchances) 18 ... ♘f6 19 ♗h4 (19 ♘g6 ♗xg3 20 ♘xh8 ♗c7 21 g4 ♘xg4↑) 19 ... 0-0 20 ♗xf6 ♖xf6 21 ♖xf6 gxf6= Eslon - Maric, Strasbourg 1972.

16 c4

16 ♕xb7 is risky because of 16 ... 0-0! 17 ♕b3 (17

♘xc6 ♖ab8!) 17 ... ♖ab8! 18 ♕xd5+ ♘xd5 with a threatening initiative for the pawn.

16 0-0 gives White nothing ♕xb3 (16 ... 0-0) 17 axb3 ♘d5!

16 0-0-0 0-0 17 c4 ♕e6 △ ... c5=

16 ...   ♕xd4

16 ... ♕a5+ 17 ♗d2 ♕c7 deserves attention.

17   c5

17 ♖d1 ♕c5

17 ♕xb7 0-0 18 ♘xc6 ♕c5! 19 ♗xd6 ♕e3+

17   ...   ♗xe5

18   ♕e6+   ♔f8

19   ♗xe5

Not 19 ♖d1? ♕xd1+! 20 ♔xd1 ♗xf4∓

19   ...   ♕e3+

With a draw by perpetual check.

A3

10   ♘e5+

This is the main line and the critical test of Black's variation.

10   ...   c6

11   d4   ♕h4+!

11 ... exd3? 12 ♗xd3 ♕b4+ 13 ♗d2 ♕e7 14 0-0-0 ♗e6 15 ♖he1±

12   g3   ♕h3

13   ♗c4

After 13 ♘xc6 Black can play 13 ... a6 14 ♗a4 ♗d7 and if 15 ♗g5 then 15 ... ♕g4! 16 ♕xg4 ♘xg4 17 d5 h6!∓ Perkins – Thales, Correspondence 1962.

13   ...   ♗e6

13 ... ♗d6 14 ♗f7+! ♔d8 (14 ... ♔e7 15 ♕b3) 15 ♗f4 ♔c7 16 ♕d2±

14   ♗g5

M. Euwe recommends 14 ♗xe6 ♕xe6 15 ♕c4. Nevertheless after 15 ... ♘d5 the position is approximately equal.

14 ♗f4 ♗d6 15 0-0-0

gives White nothing, e.g. 15 ... 0-0-0 (15 ... ♖d8 16 ♔b1 0-0 17 ♗g5 ♗xe5 18 dxe5 ♖xd1+ 19 ♖xd1 ♗xc4 20 ♕xc4+ ♘d5∓ Kramer - Rapoport, Correspondence 1973. The swift conclusion to this game was 21 ♕xe4? ♕h5 0 : 1) 16 ♗xe6+ (16 ♔b1 ♖he8 17 ♖hf1 {17 ♖he1!?} 17 ... ♗xe5? {This is a bad mistake after which White obtains a good position. Sensible alternatives for Black were 17 ... ♗xc4 18 ♕xc4 and 17 ... ♖e7!? 18 ♗b3} 18 ♗xe6+! ♕xe6 19 dxe5 ♖xd1+ 20 ♖xd1 ♘g4?! 21 ♖e1!± Popovic - Inkiov, Palma de Mallorca 1989) 16 ... ♕xe6 17 ♔b1 ♖he8 18 c4 (18 h3 h6 19 g4 c5 20 c3 cxd4 21 cxd4 ♔b8 22 ♗h2 ♖c8 23 ♖c1 ♔a8 24 ♕e3 ♗c7 25 ♖c4 ♗b8 26 ♖cc1 a6 27 ♖hd1 ♗a7 and Black was better in Hodgson - Klinger, San Bernar-

dino 1989, but he proceeded to overplay his hand and lost after 28 ♖xc8+ ♖xc8 29 ♗g1 ♕d5 30 h4 ♕xe5 31 dxe5 ♗xe3 32 exf6 ♗xg1 33 ♖xg1 gxf6 34 ♖e1 ♖e8 35 ♔c2 ♖b8 36 ♔d2 h5 37 gxh5 f5 38 ♖f1 ♖f8 39 h6 f4 40 h7 f3 41 ♖g1 1-0) 18 ... h6 19 h4 ♗xe5 20 dxe5 ♘g4! 21 ♖xd8+ ♖xd8 22 ♖d1 ♖xd1+ 23 ♕xd1 ♘xe5 24 ♕d4 ♘d3 with fine play for Black, Puig - Boey, Varna 1962.

14 ... 0-0-0

After **14 ... ♗d6** White has two ways to get a good game:

a) 15 ♖f1 ♖f8 (or 15 ... 0-0 16 ♗xf6 gxf6 17 ♗xe6+ ♕xe6 18 ♕g4+) 16 ♗xf6 gxf6 17 ♗xe6 ♕xe6 18 ♕h5+ ♔d8 19 ♘g4 Zaharov - Lipsky, Lublin 1978.

b) 15 ♗xf6 gxf6 16 ♗xe6 ♕xe6 17 ♕h5+! ♔e7 18 ♘g4 ♖ag8 (18 ... f5 19 ♘e3 ♖af8 20 d5! cxd5 21 0-0-0±) 19 ♘e3 ♖g5 20 ♕h4! ♖hg8 21 ♖f1 with a positional advantage, Vogt - Kuzmin, Leningrad 1977.

Less incisive is 15 0-0-0 which allows Black the opportunity to transpose back to the main line with 15 ... 0-0-0. However in Sherzer - Bykhovsky, Manhattan 1990, Black looked for, and found, more after 15 ... 0-0 16 g4 ♗xc4 17 ♘xc4 ♗c7 18 ♗xf6 ♖xf6 19 ♕xe4 ♗f4+ 20 ♔b1 ♕xg4 21 d5 ♕d7 22 d6 ♖e8 23 ♕d4 b5 24 ♖hf1 ♖ef8∓

15   0-0-0

15   ...   ♗d6
16   ♘f7

Following Speelman's example, the position after 15 ... ♗d6 has been the subject of a great deal of recent attention. The material available suggests that Black can face the future with confidence.

There are several other possibilities in this critical position:

a) **16 ♗xe6+** ♕xe6 17 ♘c4 ♗c7 18 ♔b1 h6 19 ♗xf6 gxf6 20 ♖hf1 f5 21 ♘e3 ♖hf8 22 ♘g2 ♖d7 23 c3 ♖g7= Bardeleben - Spielmann, Berlin 1909.

b) **16 ♗xf6** gxf6 17 ♗xe6+ ♕xe6 18 ♘c4 ♗c7 19 ♔b1 f5 20 ♘e3 ♖hf8 21 c4 f4 with equal chances, Lukov - Inkiov, Bulgaria 1982.

c) **16 g4** is an interesting attempt to cut the black queen off from the theatre of action. However, the pawn can become something of a liability, e.g. 16 ... ♗xc4 17 ♕xc4 ♖he8 18 ♘f7 ♖d7 19 d5 ♖xf7 20 dxc6 ♕xg4 21 ♗e3 ♗f4 22 ♕xf7 ♗xe3+ 23 ♔b1 bxc6 24 ♖d6 (Malaniuk - Yuferov, Sokolsky Memorial 1985) and now Black should have played 24 ... ♕g6! with good play.

Alternatively 17 ... ♗xe5 18 dxe5 ♖xd1+ 19 ♖xd1 ♕xg4 20 ♗e3! ♘d7 21 ♕f7!? (21 e6 ♘b6!) 21 ... ♘xe5 22 ♕e7 ♘g6 (22 ... ♘c4 23 ♗g5!) 23 ♕xg7 ♖d8 24 ♖xd8+ ♔xd8 25 ♕xb7 ♘e7! maintains the balance Donchev - Inkiov, Bulgaria 1989.

d) **16 ♕f1.**
As a consequence of White's debacle in Timman - Speelman, this move was recommended by various sources as the way to eliminate Black's counterplay and guarantee an advantage for White. However, it is

not clear if this assessment is justified. The material here is very interesting and worthy of close attention. 16 ... ♖he8 (16 ... ♖hf8) 17 ♕xh3 (White must exercise great caution here. The careless 17 ♗xf6? was sharply dealt with by 17 ... ♕h6+! 18 ♖d2 ♗b4 19 c3 ♖xd4! in Blatny – Klinger, Bad Worishofen 1990. Black proceeded to tidy up with 20 ♕f4 ♕xf4 21 gxf4 ♖xd2 22 ♗h4 ♗xc3 23 bxc3 e3 24 ♖e1 ♖xh2 25 ♘f3 ♖g2 26 ♖xe3 ♗f7 27 ♖xe8+ ♗xe8 28 ♗e1 b5 29 ♗g8 ♗g6 30 ♗e6+ ♔c7 31 f5 ♗e8 32 ♗d2 ♗d7 33 ♗f4+ ♔d8 34 ♗d6 h5 35 ♘e5 ♗xe6 36 fxe6 h4 37 ♘xc6+ ♔e8 38 ♘d4 a6 39 e7 ♖g6 40 ♘f5 h3 41 a4 bxa4 42 ♗c7 ♖g2 43 ♗d8 ♔d7 44 ♘d6 ♖e2 0-1) 17 ... ♗xh3 18 ♘f7 ♖d7 19 ♘xd6+ ♖xd6 20 ♗f4 ♖d7 21 ♖he1 ♗g4 22 ♖d2

♘d5 23 ♗e5 ♗f3 24 ♖f2 and with the plan of c3 and ♗d3 White had a very pleasant position, Sax – Inkiov, Rome 1984. This served to put players off the black side of this variation for some time. It is rather ironic that Speelman resurrected a line that had put out of commission by this game, as Sax was one of Timman's seconds in the match!

Practice has witnessed two deviations from the above game:

a) 20 ♖he1 ♗g4 21 ♖d2 ♘d5 (This doesn't work out too well. 21 ... b5(!) maintaining tension is an alternative which should be considered) 22 ♗e2 ♗xe2 23 ♖dxe2 ♖de6 24 a3 b5 25 ♔d2 ♔c7 26 b3 h6 27 ♗f4+ ♘xf4 28 gxf4 ♔d6 29 c4 bxc4 30 bxc4 ♖b8 31 ♔c3 ♖be8 32 f5 ♖f6 33 ♖xe4 ♖xe4 34 ♖xe4 ♖xf5 35 ♖e8 ♖f2 36 c5+ ♔c7 37 ♖e7+ ♔b8 38 ♖xg7 ♖xh2 39 ♔b4 ♖d2 40 ♖d7 h5 41 ♔a5 h4 42 ♔a6 ♖a2 43 ♖b7+ ♔c8 44 ♖b3 ♖g2 45 ♔xa7 ♖g3 46 ♖b8+ ♔d7 47 ♖b7+ ♔e6 48 ♖h7 ♖xa3+ 49 ♔b6 ♔d5 50 ♖h5+ ♔xd4 51 ♖xh4+ 1-0 Zilberstein – Tsarev, Kiev 1989.

b) 23 ... e3!? was Inkiov's

own contribution – 24 ♖d3
♘b6 25 ♕b3 e2 26 ♖e3 (26
h3? ♗xh3 27 ♖xe2 ♗f1) 26 ...
a5 27 a4 c5! 28 c3 (28 ♖c3
♖xe5!!) 28 ... c4 29 ♗c2 ♘d5
30 ♖e4 ♗f3 31 ♖h4? g5! 32
♖xh7 ♘e3 33 ♖xd7 ♔xd7 34
♗g6? ♖e6! 35 ♕b1 ♘g2 36
♖xe2 ♗xe2 37 ♗f5 ♗d3 38
♗xe6+ ♔xe6-+ Ernst – In-
kiov Gausdal 1989.

16   ...   ♗xf7
17   ♗xf7   ♖hf8
18   ♗c4

18 ♗b3 ♖de8 19 c4 ♕g4 20
♕e3 ♘h5 21 ♖df1 ♖xf1+ 22
♖xf1 h6 23 c5 ♗xg3 24 hxg3
♕xg5= was Velimirovic –
Klinger, Palma de Mallorca
1989

18   ...   ♖de8
19   d5

19 ♖hf1 h6 (19 ... ♔b8!?)
20 ♗f4 ♗xf4+ 21 ♖xf4
(Yudovich – Boey, Corres-
pondence 1972/76). Here
Black equalised with 21 ...

♖e7! as 22 d5 would be met
by 22 ... cxd5 23 ♗xd5 ♖fe8
with a reasonable position.

19   ...   c5

Black now stands very
well and conducts the re-
mainder of the game with
extreme accuracy.

20   ♖hf1   ♔b8
21   ♗f4   ♖d8
22   ♗g5   a6!
23   ♗xf6   gxf6
24   ♕xe4   ♕xh2

White is very exposed on
the dark squares and his
bishop is severely handi-
capped by the pawn on d5.
In an attempt to simplify
the situation he now in-
augurates a pawn exchange
on the kingside while ad-
vancing his rook to the
seventh rank. However, this
weakens his own back rank,
and Speelman swiftly
pounces.

25   ♖h1   ♕xg3
26   ♖xh7   ♖fe8
27   ♕f5   b5!

Suddenly its all over. 28
♗d3 c4 is no improvement
for White.

28   ♗f1   ♖e1
29   ♕h5   ♕f4+
       0 : 1

Timman – Speelman, Can-
didates Semi-Final, London
1989.

Speelman psyched him-self up for the games in this match by looking at book containing pictures of wolves. This plan had yielded little success (one loss and five draws) prior to this demolition. When asked to explain this, Jon pointed out that this game was played on a day when there was a full moon!

B

	9	...	♕h4+
	10	g3	♕h3

In this gambit continua-tion, Black has definite positional compensation, due to the weaknesses in the White position. We now examine two possible res-ponses:

B1) 11 ♘xa7+
B2) 11 ♘e5+

B1

    11 ♘xa7+ ♗d7

11 ... ♔d8 12 ♘xc8 ♔xc8 is worth a look.

    12 ♗xd7+ ♕xd7

An interesting alterna-tive which has not yet been seen in practice is **12 ... ♘xd7!?** 13 ♕xe4+ ♗e7 14 ♕xb7 0-0 with a dangerous attack for the sacrificed pawns.

    13 ♘b5

With the further dicho-tomy:

B11) 13 ... 0-0-0
B12) 13 ... c6

B11

    13 ... 0-0-0

see following diagram

    14 b3

14 0-0 is dangerous after 14 ... ♗c5+ 15 ♔h1 h5!↑

The continuations **14 ♘c3 c6** and **14 ♛c4 c6 15 ♘c3 h5** lead to positions examined in C2aii.

14   ...   ♗c5

14 ... c6 is inaccurate, e.g. **15 ♘a3!** and now:

a) **15 ... ♗b4 16 ♘c4 ♔b8 17 ♗b2** and White will consolidate the material advantage.

b) **15 ... b5 16 ♗b2 ♛a7 17 ♘xb5!** cxb5 18 ♛xb5 with more than sufficient compensation.

c) **15 ... ♛d4** - see game no. 8, Estrin - Neishtadt.

15   ♗b2   ♘g4
16   ♖f1

Estrin considered that White should play **16 0-0-0 ♘f2 17 ♛c4** and if **17 ... ♘xd1 18 ♖xd1 ♛d5** (18 ... ♗b6 19 ♗e5) 19 ♛a4 ♔b8 20 ♗e5 ♗b6 21 ♘c3± Stronger, however, is **17 ... ♗b6!** 18 ♖he1 (18 ♗e5 ♘xh1) 18 ...

♘xd1 19 ♖xd1 e3! 20 d4 ♖he8 getting a positional edge.

16   ...   c6

In this position Black has dangerous threats in return for the two sacrificed pawns.

17   ♘c3

17 ♘a3 e3 18 d4 (18 0-0-0 exd2+ 19 ♖xd2 ♗e3 20 ♛xe3 ♘xe3 21 ♖xd7 ♖xd7 22 ♖e1 ♖hd8 23 ♗xg7 ♖d1+ 24 ♖xd1 ♖xd1+ 25 ♔b2 ♖h1∓) 18 ... ♗xa3 19 ♗xa3 ♛xd4 20 ♛xg4+ ♔b8 21 ♔e2 ♛d2+ 22 ♔f3 ♖he8! 23 c4 ♖d3! with a decisive attack.

17   ...   e3
18   d3   ♘f2!
19   ♛f3   ♗b4
20   ♔e2   ♖he8

Black has an active position with strong threats.

B12

13   ...   c6

14 ♘c3

On 14 ♘a3 Black can profitably reply 14 ... b5.

14 ... 0-0-0

15 b3

Others:

a) **15 ♛c4** h5 16 h4 ♛g4 17 ♘e2 ♘d5 18 ♛xe4 (18 a3 was played in Bikova – Zvorikina, Moscow 1959, and now with 18 ... ♖h6! 19 b4 {19 b3 b5} 19 ... ♖hd6 20 ♗b2 ♘b6! 21 ♛c3 ♘a4) 18 ... ♖h6 19 ♖f1 ♖e6 20 ♛f3 ♖de8 (20 ... ♛f5 21 d3 ♘b4!) 21 ♛xg4 hxg4 22 ♖f2 ♗c5 23 ♖g2 ♘b4 and White has difficult problems to solve.

b) **15 a4** ♗b4 (15 ... h5! at once may be better, e.g. 16 h4 ♗b4 17 a5 e3 18 dxe3 ♘e4∓ Durao – Boey, Hague 1966) 16 ♘d1 h5 17 c3 ♗d6 18 ♘e3 h4 19 ♘c4 ♚c7 20 ♘xd6 ♛xd6 21 ♖g1 hxg3 22 hxg3 ♛c5↑ Postnikov – Ergle, 1966.

15 ... ♗b4
16 ♗b2

16 a3 allows Black excellent chances after 16 ... ♗xc3 17 dxc3 e3! For example: 18 ♗xe3 18 ... ♖he8 19 0-0 ♘d5 20 ♖f3 ♛g4 with the initiative, or 18 0-0 ♖he8 19 ♗b2 ♛g4! and it is not easy for White to defend himself.

16 ... e3!
17 0-0-0 exd2+
18 ♚b1

18 ♖xd2 ♛xd2+ 19 ♛xd2 ♖xd2 20 ♚xd2 ♘e4+ 21 ♚d3 ♘f2+–+

18 ... ♖he8
19 ♛c4

In this position Black's advantage is not in doubt as can be seen from the following examples.

19 ... ♛e7

19 ... ♗xc3 20 ♗xc3 b5 21 ♛f1 ♘e4 22 ♗a5 ♛a7 23 ♗xd8 ♘c3+ 24 ♚b2 ♛d4–+

Romanov - Bebchuk, Moscow 1962.

20	♘a4	♘g4
21	♗d4	♖xd4!
22	♛xd4	♖d8
23	♛g1	♘e3
24	♘b2	♛e4
25	♘d3	♖xd3!
	0 : 1	

Oliyane - Sanches, Correspondence 1975/76.

B2

11	♘e5+	c6
12	♗c4	♗c5

12 ... ♗e6 13 b3 (13 c3 ♗e7 △ 14 ... 0-0) 13 ... ♗c5 14 ♗b2 0-0-0?! (14 ... 0-0 is worthy of attention, in order to answer 15 0-0-0 with 15 ... b5) 15 0-0-0 ♖he8 16 ♗xe6+ ♛xe6 17 ♖he1! h5 18 ♛c4 ♖d5 19 ♛f1 ♛f5 20 d3±

12 ... h5!? - see game no. 9 Kuntselman - Nesterenko.

White has an extra pawn, but has weaknesses in his position. Black has good chances to organise active counterplay.

Now two continuations come into consideration:

B21) 13 c3
B22) 13 d3

Alternatives give White little, e.g. 13 ♗f7+ ♚d8 14 d4 ♗xd4 15 ♛d2 c5 16 c3 e3!∓ Chutger - Selivanovsky, Moscow 1956, or 13 d4 ♗xd4 14 ♗f7+ (14 ♘e3 ♗xe5! 15 fxe5 ♗g4!) 14 ... ♚e7 (14 ... ♚d8) 15 ♘e3 ♗xe5 16 fxe5 ♚xf7 17 exf6 ♖d8! 18 fxg7 ♗g4 19 ♛c4+ ♚xg7 20 ♛xe4 ♖e8 21 ♛f4 ♖ad8 22 ♛g5+ ♚h8 23 ♛f6+ with perpetual, Radev - Kirov, Sofia 1974.

B21

13 c3

Euwe's recommendation.

13 ...   ♗f5!

13 ... ♘g4? 14 d4 ♘xe5 15 fxe5 ♗e7 16 ♖f1! ♗f5 17 ♖f2! ♖f8 18 ♗e3 0-0-0 19 ♕f1!± Bagirov – Shahtahtinsky, Correspondence 1966.

14 d4

On **14 b4** Black answers 14 ... ♗b6. The correspondence game Kolarov – Boey, 1971 continued 15 b5 (better looks 15 ♗a3 0-0-0 16 0-0-0 ♘g4 17 b5 as in the game Bak – Hebel, Berlin 1975 but then with 17 ... cxb5! 18 ♗xb5 ♘f2! Black obtains good counterchances) 15 ... 0-0-0 16 bxc6 ♘g4! 17 ♗a3 ♗f2+ 18 ♔d1 ♘xe5 19 ♕xf2 e3! and Black has real threats.

14 ...   exd3

15 ♘xd3+

15 ♗xd3 0-0-0 16 ♗xf5+ (16 ♗e3? ♗xd3 17 ♘xd3 ♖xd3! 18 ♕xd3 ♗xe3 19 ♖f1 ♕e6 0 : 1 Krasov – Lipsky, Slyupsk 1977) 16 ... ♕xf5 17 ♗e3 ♕e4 18 ♔f2 ♕xe3+ 19 ♕xe3 ♖d2+ 20 ♔f3 ♗xe3 21 ♔xe3 ♖xb2 ½ : ½ Leonidov – Shikirev, Moscow 1977.

15 ...   ♗e7

16 ♘e5

Alternatives:

a) **16 ♘f2** ♕g2 17 ♕f1 ♕f3 18 ♕e2 ♕g2 led to a draw in Browne – Kavalek, USA 1973.

b) **16 ♗e3** 0-0-0 17 0-0-0 ♗g4 18 ♕c2 ♗xd1 19 ♖xd1 b5 20 ♗b3 ♔b7 21 ♗g1 ♘d7 22 ♖e1 ♗d6 and Black consolidated his extra pawn in the correspondence game Nechesany – Boey, 1976.

c) **16 ♗d2** b5! (in Hennings – Westerinen, 1965 the weak reply 16 ... 0-0-0? led to a white advantage after 17 0-0-0 ♘e4 {17 ... ♖he8 18 ♘f2} 18 ♘f2 ♘xf2 19 ♕xf2 ♔b8 20 ♗e3) 17 ♗b3 ♗e4! 18 ♘f2 ♕g2 19 0-0-0 (Melegeghyi suggests 19 ♕f1 however after 19 ... ♗c5 20 ♕xg2 ♗xg2 21 ♖g1 ♗f3 22 ♗d1 ♗d5 Black has a good game) 19 ... ♗c5 20 ♗e3 (20 ♗e1? ♕f3) 20 ... ♗f3 21 ♕d3 ♗xd1 22 ♗xc5 (22 ♗xd1 ♖d8 23 ♕e2 ♗xe3+ 24 ♕xe3+ ♔f7 25 ♗b3+ ♘d5 Black's position is preferable) 22 ... ♗xb3 23 ♖e1+ (23 axb3 ♕d5 24 ♕e3+ ♔f7 25 ♕e7+ ♔g6) 23 ... ♔f7 24 ♖e7+ ♔g8 25 axb3 ♕d5∓

16 ...   0-0-0

17 ♗e3

Others:

17 ♘f7? is a mistake, e.g. 17 ... ♗g4! 18 ♘xd8 ♖xd8! (Florian).

17 ♗d2 ♗c5 (17 ... ♘g4 18 0-0-0 ♗c5!) 18 0-0-0 ♘g4!

(18 ... ♖he8 19 ♕f1 {19 ♗f7!
♗d3 20 ♕f3 ♗e4 21 ♕f1 ♕f5
22 ♕c4 ♗xh1 23 ♕xc5 ♗e4
24 ♕xa7 ♖e7 25 c4 ♖xd2 26
♖xd2 ♘d7 27 ♗e8!± Sorokin
- Spodny, correspondence
1977/80} 19 ... ♘e4! 20 ♕xh3
♗xh3 21 ♖he1 ♘f2∓ Cording
- Boey, correspondence
1965/66) 19 ♕f3 ♘f2 20 ♖he1
(Hazai - Szell, Budapest
1973) 20 ... ♘xd1! 21 ♗a6
♖d5! 22 ♘xc6 ♖d7 and
White has no compensation
for the sacrificed material
(Euwe).

| 17 | ... | ♘g4 |
| 18 | ♘xg4 | |

18 ♗xa7? ♘xe5 19 fxe5
♗g4 (also good is 19 ... ♗g5
20 ♗e3 ♗xe3 21 ♕xe3 ♕g2)
20 ♕e4 ♖hf8 21 ♗f1 ♗g5! 22
♗d4 ♕h5 23 ♗e2 ♖xd4! 24
cxd4 ♗xe2 25 ♕xe2 ♖f3 and
Black went on to win in
Gelensky - Boey, corres-
pondence 1965/66.

18	...	♗xg4
19	♕f1	♕h5
20	♕f2	♗c5!

see following diagram

21 0-0!
Capturing with 21 ♗xc5 is
mistaken, e.g. 21 ... ♖he8+
22 ♗e3 (22 ♔f1 ♗h3+ 23 ♔g1
♖d1+ 24 ♖xd1 ♕xd1+ 25 ♗f1

♖e1↑) 22 ... ♖xe3+ 23 ♕xe3
♖e8 24 ♕xe8+ ♕xe8+ 25 ♔f2
♕e4-+

21	...	♗xe3
22	♕xe3	♖he8
23	♕xa7	♗e2!
24	♗xe2	♖xe2
25	♖f2=	

Cording - Boey, corres-
pondence 1974/75.

B22
| 13 | d3 |

This continuation is re-
liable, and for a long time
proved good for White.

13 ... ♘g4

13 ... exd3!? deserves attention, e.g. 14 ♘xd3+ ♗e7 15 ♘e5 ♗f5 with definate compensation for the pawn. In Browne - Minic, Mannheim 1975, Black played 13 ... ♗f5 at once and after 14 ♗e3 exd3 15 ♗xd3 ♗xe3 16 ♛xe3 ♘d5 17 ♗xf5 ♛xf5 18 ♛d3 0-0 19 ♛xf5 ♖xf5 20 ♘d3 White had an extra pawn without any real compensation for Black.

14 ♘f7!

A strong move. White gets nothing with **14 d4** ♗xd4 15 ♛xe4 ♘xe5 16 fxe5. Karpov - Parma, Ljubliana - Portoroz 1975 saw 16 ... ♛g4 17 ♛xg4 ♗xg4 18 c3 ♗xe5 19 0-0 0-0-0= Black could have played more ambitiously, e.g. 16 ... ♗g4! 17 c3 (17 ♛xd4 ♖d8 18 ♛e4 ♖d1+ 19 ♔f2 ♖f8+↑) 17 ... ♗c5 18 b4 ♗b6 19 ♗f4 Gudim - Selivanovsky, Liepaya 1971. Now with Tal's suggestion of 19 ... ♖f8! 20 e6 g5! 21 e7 ♖xf4! 22 gxf4 ♛xc3+ Black could have obtained a winning position.

Zak has suggested **14 ♛xe4** as being good for White, with the following analysis - 14 ... ♘f2 15 ♛e2

(15 ♗f7+ - see game no. 10 Heemsoth - Konstantino-polsky) 15 ... ♘xh1 16 ♘g6+ ♔d7! 17 ♘xh8 ♗f2+ (17 ... b5!? 18 ♗b3 a5 looks preferable) 18 ♔d2 b5 19 ♗b3 ♛xh2 20 ♛e6+ (20 ♔c3 a5!) 20 ... ♔c7 21 ♛e5+ ♔b7 (21 ... ♔b6!? 22 ♔c3) 22 ♛e7+ ♔b8! 23 ♛d6+ and White has nothing better than repetition, as 23 ♘f7 leads to better chances for Black after 23 ... ♗d4+ 24 ♛e2 ♛xe2+ 25 ♔xe2 ♗g4+.

14 ... ♗f2+
15 ♔d1 e3

15 ... ♘e3+ 16 ♗xe3 ♗g4 17 ♗xf2 is unsatisfactory. White has more than sufficient compensation for the queen.

16 ♛f3

16 ♘xh8? is mistaken, e.g. 16 ... ♘h6! 17 ♗xe3 ♗g4 and Black wins the white queen in a favourable situation.

16 ... ♘f6
Others:

a) **16 ... ♘xh2** 17 ♛e4+ ♔f8 18 ♗xe3 ♗g4+ 19 ♔d2 ♖e8 20 ♘e5 ♛xg3 21 ♗xf2 ♛xf2+ 22 ♔c3 g6 23 ♖xh2! ♛xh2 24 ♛d4!+- proved decisive in Kavalek - Ljubojevic, Amsterdam 1975.

b) **16 ... ♘h6!?**

and White has various possible responses:

bi) 17 ♘d6+ ♔d7 18 ♗xe3 ♕g4 and White loses material.

bii) 17 ♘xh6 gxh6 18 ♕e4+ ♔f8 19 ♗xe3 (19 c3 b5) 19 ... ♗g4+ 20 ♔d2 ♖e8 21 ♗xf2 ♖xe4 22 dxe4 ♕g2 23 ♖hf1 reaches a position which Maric assesses as unclear. Indeed, after 23 ... ♕xe4 24 ♗c5+ ♔g7 25 ♗d3 ♕d5 26 ♗b4 ♖e8 27 ♗c3+ ♔f8 a situation of dynamic equality arises.

biii) 17 ♘e5 can lead to an immediate repetition by 17 ... ♘g4 18 ♘f7, but Black can try 17 ... ♘f5, e.g. 18 c3 h5 19 ♔c2 h4, 18 g4 ♗xf3+ 19 ♘xf3 ♘h4 20 ♘e5 ♘g2 or 18 ♕e4 ♘d6 19 ♕f3 ♘xc4!? (19 ... ♘f5) 20 dxc4 0-0 21 ♗xe3 ♗xe3 22 ♕xe3 ♕g2 – in all cases with sufficient compensation for the sacrificed material.

biv) 17 ♕e4+ ♔f8 18 ♗xe3 ♗xe3! (18 ... ♗g4+ 19 ♔d2 ♖e8 20 ♘e5±) 19 ♕xe3 ♘xf7 20 ♕c5+ (20 ♖e1 ♕d7) 20 ... ♔g8 21 ♖e1 ♗g4+ 22 ♔d2 ♕xh2+ 23 ♔c3 ♕h5 24 ♖e5 ♕g6 25 ♖e7 ♕f6+! 26 ♔d2 (26 ♔b3 ♖f8 27 ♖ae1 b5!) 26 ... ♖f8 27 ♖ae1 h6 28 ♖xb7 g5!∓

17   f5

17 ♘d6+ ♔d7 18 ♘xc8 ♖e8! led to Black's advantage in Sunye Neto – Boey, Nice 1974.

A critical position.

17   ...   ♘d5!

17 ... ♖f8 18 ♘d6+ (stronger is 18 ♗xe3! ♕g4 19 ♘d6+ ♔d7 20 ♔e2 ♕xf3+ 21 ♔xf3 ♗xe3 22 ♘xc8 ♗c5 23 ♗e6+ ♔c7 24 d4 ♗xd4 25 c3 which Maric suggests is very good for White, but this assessment should be challenged as after 25 ...

♘d7 26 cxd4 ♖axc8 27 ♗xd7
♚xd7 Black preserves
chances for a draw) 18 ...
♚d7 19 ♘xc8 ♘d5! 20 ♘e7
(20 ♗xd5 ♖xf5 21 ♛e4
♖e5!!-+) 20 ... ♖ae8 21 ♗xd5
cxd5 22 ♗xe3 ♗xe3 23 ♖e1
♖xe7 24 ♖xe3 ♖xe3 25
♛xd5+ and this position
was shortly agreed drawn
in Nunn – Rumens, London
1977.

18	♗xd5	cxd5
19	♘d6+	♚d7
20	♘xc8	♖e8

21	♛xd5+	♚xc8
22	♚e2?	

Here it was necessary to
beat a retreat and conclude
the game as a draw with 22
♛e5+ ♚d7 23 ♛d4+ ♚c8.
White's ambition proves to
be immediately fatal.

22	...	♛g4+
23	♛f3	♛a4
24	b3	♛d4
25	♖b1	♛c3
	0 : 1	

Balashov – Hramov, corr-
espondence 1986/89

11) Illustrative Games

Illustrative game 1
Teichmann – Marshall
Monte Carlo 1903

1	e4	e5
2	♘f3	♘c6
3	♗b5	f5
4	♘c3	♘f6
5	♕e2	♘d4
6	♘xd4	exd4
7	e5	

In the event of 7 exf5+ Black must reply 7 ... ♗e7 8 ♘e4 0-0 with an initiative for the sacrificed pawn. 7 ... ♔f7? is a mistake after 8 ♕c4+, and 7 ... ♕e7 also leads to a White advantage after 8 ♕xe7+ ♗xe7 9 ♘e2.

7	...	♘g4
8	h3	♘h6
9	♘b1	

9 ♘d1 (Spassky – Bisguier, Goteborg 1955) was examined in the theoretical section.

9	...	♕g5
10	0-0	c6
11	♗c4	f4
12	d3	d5!
13	exd6+	♔d8!

This idea of the American player Atkins, was seen for the first time in this game. Black gets an active position for the pawn.

14	♘d2!	

Necessary. Bringing this knight to e4 is an integral part of the White defence.

14	...	♗xh3
15	♕f3	♗f5

15 ... ♗g4 would obvious-

ly be met by 16 ♘e4 ♗xf3 17 ♘xg5±

16	♘e4	♕xe4
17	dxe4	♗xd6
18	c3!	

Black has an extra pawn, but his king is held up in the centre. White hurries to exploit this by opening the central files.

18	...	d3!

Forced. 18 ... dxc3? leads to an immediate win for White after 19 ♖d1 ♔c7 20 ♖xd6!

19	♖d1	♔c7
20	♖xd3	♖hf8
21	g3	♕g6

Black now threatens ... ♖ad8 consolidating the position, followed by the regrouping of the knight on h6 to a more relevant square.

White must therefore take decisive measures and to this end Teichmann sac-rifices the exchange to maintain the initiative.

22	♖xd6!	♔xd6

The tempting 22 ... ♕xd6 23 ♗xf4 ♔c8 is refuted by 24 ♗xd6 ♖xf3 25 ♗f4! △ 26 ♗e2.

23	♗xf4+	♔e7
24	♕e3	

White has a dangerous attack as compensation for the exchange.

24	...	♘g4!

The only defence. Black commences a counterattack against the central point e5.

25	♕c5+	♔e8
26	♗g5	♕xe4

Again forced.

27	♕b4!	♘xf2

Black threatens mate on h1 and at the same time defends the queen.

28	♔h2	♘g4+
29	♔h3	♘f2+

½ : ½

It is clear that White cannot avoid perpetual check.

Illustrative game 2
Boleslavsky – Tolush
Moscow 1957

1	e4	e5
2	♘f3	♘c6
3	♗b5	f5

4	♘c3	♘f6
5	exf5	♘d4
6	♗a4	♗c5

Boleslavsky later admitted that the opening employed by Tolush came as a complete surprise to him.

7	d3	0-0

Black's seventh is a flexible continuation. Now if 8 ♘e4 there may follow 8 ... ♘xe4 9 dxe4 d5! with a dangerous initiative.

8	0-0	d5
9	♘xe5	♗xf5
10	♗g5	♕d6

As seen earlier, 10 ... c6 is more precise.

11	♖e1	c6
12	♗h4	♖ae8
13	♗g3	♕d8
14	♘e2	

The following unexpected, but well-founded exchange sacrifice, enables Black to develop the initiative.

14	...	♖xe5!
15	♗xe5	♗g4
16	♕d2	

Feeling seriously threatened by the danger to his king, Boleslavsky returns the exchange intending to simplify. The attempt to hold on to the extra material would have been misguided, e.g. 16 ♗xd4 ♗xd4 17 c3 ♗b6 18 d4 ♘e4! 19 ♖f1 (19 f3 ♗xf3 20 gxf3 ♕g5+ 21 ♘g3 ♘xg3 22 hxg3 ♕xg3+-+) 19 ... ♗c7 20 ♕d3 ♗xh2+ 21 ♔xh2 ♕h4+ 22 ♔g1 ♘xf2 23 ♖xf2 ♕xf2+ 24 ♔h1 ♖f6 25 ♘g1 ♖h6+ 26 ♘h3 ♖xh3+ 27 gxh3 ♗f3+-+

16	...	♘xe2+
17	♖xe2	♗xe2
18	♕xe2	

White seems to have good chances to repulse the enemy threats and retain an extra pawn, but

Black is better developed and immediately exploits this.

18	...	♘e4!
19	♖f1!	

This is forced, as 19 dxe4 ♖xf2 20 ♕xf2 ♗xf2+ 21 ♔xf2 ♕b6+! 22 ♔f3 ♕b4 wins for Black and 19 d4 ♖xf2 20 ♕g4 ♕e7 is also unattractive.

19	...	♖xf2
20	♖xf2	♗xf2+
21	♔f1	♕f8!

Now White must capture the enemy knight resulting in an equal ending.

22	dxe4	♗d4+
23	♕f3	♗xe5
	½ : ½	

After 24 ♕xf8+ ♔xf8 25 exd5 cxd5 26 ♗b3! the draw is obvious.

Illustrative game 3
Diaz - Salkedo
Correspondence 1985

1	e4	e5
2	♘f3	♘c6
3	♗b5	f5
4	♘c3	♘f6
5	exf5	♗c5
6	0-0	0-0
7	♘xe5	♘d4
8	♗a4	

As seen earlier, 8 ♘f3 at once is preferable.

8	...	d5
9	♘f3	

Too late. Now Black can develop the initiative without hindrance. For 9 d3 ♗xf5 see the previous game.

9	...	♗xf5
10	♘xd4	♗xd4
11	♘e2	

There is nothing better as after 11 ♘b5 ♗g4 12 ♕e1 ♖e8 White loses the queen, and if 11 d3 ♘g4! with a tremendous attack. However the move played also fails to solve all White's difficulties.

11	...	♗g4
12	♕e1	c6!

With the aim of eliminating the bishop's influence on e8. If now 13 ♘xd4? then 13 ... ♖e8, and on 13 h3? will follow 13 ... ♗xe2 14 ♕xe2 ♘e4 threatening ... ♘g3.

13	c3	♖e8
14	♗d1	

Bad is 14 cxd4 because of 14 ... ♘xe2 and White suffers material loss.

14 ... ♖e6

This is more exact than 14 ... ♘xe2 15 ♗xe2 ♕e7 16 cxd4 ♕xe2 17 ♕xe2 ♖xe2 18 d3. Black follows the well-known principle that, when attacking, the queen should be placed behind the rook.

15	cxd4	♘xe2
16	♗xe2	♕e7
17	d3	

17 f3 ♘h5!

17	...	♖xe2
18	♕c3	♕d6!

An improvement over 18 ... ♖e8 19 ♗f4! (Grinberg - Szmetan, Argentinian Ch. 1973) when White will follow up with the useful blockading move ♗e5.

19 g3

19 ♗e3 loses to 19 ... ♖e8 20 ♖ae1 (20 h3 ♖8xe3! 21 fxe3 ♕xg3) 20 ... ♘g4! 21 g3 ♖8xe3! 22 fxe3 ♖xh2 23 ♖f3 ♕h6 with an inevitable mate.

19	...	♖ae8
20	♗g5?	

Losing, but after the comparatively better 20 ♗f4 ♕e6 21 ♗e5 ♘g4 22 ♖ae1 ♘xe5! 23 dxe5 ♖xe5 24 ♖xe5 ♕xe5 Black stands very well.

20	...	♘g4!
21	♖ae1	♘xf2!
22	♖xe2	♘h3+
23	♔g2	♖xe2+
24	♔xh3	♕e6+
25	g4	h5!
26	♖g1	♕f7!!
	0 : 1	

Illustrative game 4
Chiburdanidze - Gaprindashvili
Rostov 1980

1	e4	e5
2	♘f3	♘c6
3	♗b5	f5
4	♘c3	♘d4
5	0-0	♘xb5

The usual move here is 5 ... c6. Black decided instead to remove the 'Spanish' bishop - a decision that led to difficulties.

6 ♘xb5 fxe4

6 ... d6 can be met by 7 exf5! ♗xf5 8 d4 e4 9 ♘g5 and if 9 ... h6 then 10 ♘xe4 ♗xe4 11 ♖e1±

7 ♘xe5

see following diagram

It is only necessary to glance at this position to realise that with the White lead in development, Black will experience difficulties

here.

	7	...	♘e7

7 ... ♘f6 8 ♘g4! ♗e7 (8 ... ♘xg4 9 ♕xg4 d5 10 ♕h5+) 9 ♘xf6+ ♗xf6 10 ♕h5+ ♔f8 (10 ... g6 11 ♕d5) 11 ♕c5+ d6 12 ♕xc7± Psakhis – Kozlov, 1980.

	8	♕h5+	g6
	9	♕h4	♗g7
	10	♕f4	

Before capturing the pawn, White deprives her opponent of the right to castle.

	10	...	♖f8
	11	♕xe4	d6
	12	♘f3	♗f5
	13	♕c4	c6
	14	♘bd4	d5
	15	♕e2	♕d7
	16	♘xf5	♕xf5
	17	♖e1	♗f6
	18	♘d4	

With an extra pawn and better position, White has a decisive advantage. The remainder is a mopping up operation.

	18	...	♕d7
	19	♘e6	♖f7
	20	d4	♖c8
	21	c3	b6
	22	♗g5	c5
	23	♗xf6	♖xf6
	24	♕e5	1 : 0

Illustrative game 5
Karpov – Mark Tseitlin
Leningrad 1971

	1	e4	e5
	2	♘f3	♘c6
	3	♗b5	f5
	4	♘c3	♘d4
	5	♗a4	♘f6
	6	♘xe5	fxe4
	7	0-0	♗c5

At the time of this game it was not yet known that Black can obtain good play with the unusual move 7 ... ♗d6!

8	♘xe4	♘xe4
9	♕h5+	g6
10	♘xg6	

10	...	♘f6?

This is already the decisive mistake. Necessary was 10 ... ♕g5! 11 ♕xg5 ♘xg5 12 ♖e1+ ♘ge6! (commentators had only considered 12 ... ♘de6? here) 13 ♘xh8 b5 14 ♗b3 ♔f8 and Black will get counterplay.

11	♕e5+!	♗e7
12	♘xh8	b5
13	♕xd4	bxa4
14	♖e1	♔f8
15	d3	

Now that the knight on h8 is invulnerable, White has a material and positional advantage.

15	...	♖b8

15 ... ♔g7 would be met by 16 ♗f4! d6 (16 ... ♕f8 17 ♕e3!; 16 ... ♗d6 17 ♗h6+!

♔xh8 18 ♖e8+! ♕xe8 19 ♕xf6+ and mate next move) 17 ♖e3 and Black cannot take the knight because of 18 ♖ae1 ♗d6 19 ♖e8.

16	♕e5!	

Now Black's king is tied to the defence of the bishop at e7 and his position is hopeless.

16	...	♘g8

There is nothing better, e.g. 16 ... ♖b6 17 ♗h6+ ♔e8 18 ♕g5.

17	♕h5	♔g7
18	♘f7	♕e8
19	♗h6+	♘xh6
20	♕xh6+	♔xf7

Black at last captures the enemy knight, but finds his king exposed to a mating attack.

21	♕xh7+	♔f8
22	♖e3	♖b6
23	♖g3!	1 : 0

Illustrative game 6
Kalegin - Mik. Tseitlin
Ryazan 1986

1	e4	e5
2	♘f3	♘c6
3	♗b5	f5
4	♘c3	fxe4
5	♘xe4	♘f6
6	♘xf6+	♕xf6
7	♕e2	♗e7
8	0-0	♘d4
9	♘xd4	exd4
10	♖e1	c6
11	♗d3	d5
12	b3	0-0
13	♕xe7	♕xf2+
14	♔h1	♗h3
15	♖g1	♖ae8
16	♕xf8+	

The psychological background to this game is interesting. On his fifteenth move, White could have forced a draw with 15 gxh3, but Kalegin knew the correspondence game Yavorsky - Gartner, 1980/82, where the continuation 15 ♖g1 ♖ae8 16 ♕xf8+ ♖xf8 17 ♘a3 ♖e8 18 ♖af1 ♕xd2 19 gxh3 ♕a5 20 ♘d6 led to a White victory. Obviously hoping to emulate this success, he chose to repeat this variation, but was met by an unpleasant surprise.

16 ...   ♕xf8!

Here is the value of home preparation! This significant improvement was voted one of the best twelve theoretical novelties of *Informator 41*. Now White has to solve difficult problems at the board.

17   ♖f1   ♗xg2+
18   ♔xg2   ♕d6!

Precisely the right moment. In the as yet unpublished correspondence game Rabinovich - Sauerman 1981/86, Black played the inferior 18 ... ♕e7 and after 19 ♗b2 ♕g5+ 20 ♔h1 c5 21 ♖f5 White was better.

19   ♗b2   c5
20   ♖f2

Exchanging rooks by 20 ♖ae1 ♖xe1 21 ♖xe1 ♕f4 does not reduce Black's pressure.

20 ...   ♖f8!

A difficult decision. After long thought, Black

concluded that it was now necessary to exchange one pair of rooks as after 20 ... b5 21 ♗xb5 (or 21 ♖af1 c4 22 ♗f5 g6) 21 ... ♕g6+ 22 ♔h1 ♕e4+ 23 ♖g2 the position is unclear, and 20 ... c4 21 bxc4 ♕b6 22 ♗a3 ♕a6 23 ♖e1! leads to good play for White.

| 21 | ♖af1 | ♖xf2+ |
| 22 | ♖xf2 | b5 |

23 b4

23 ♗xb5? ♕g6+ 24 ♔f1 ♕xc2.

| 23 | ... | c4 |
| 24 | ♘f5 | g6 |

Not 24 ... ♕e5? because of 25 ♘xd4! ♕xd4 26 ♗e6+.

25	♗g4	♕e5
26	♗f3	h5!
27	♖e2	♕g5+
28	♔h1	♕f5
29	♔g2	

29 ♗g2 ♕xc2 30 ♗xd5+ ♔h7 31 ♖e7+ ♔h6 32 ♗xd4 ♕d1+ 33 ♗g1 c3! also leads

to a decisive advantage for Black.

| 29 | ... | ♕g5+ |
| 30 | ♔f1 | |

30 ♔h1 ♕f5 31 ♔g2 g5!

30	...	♕f5
31	♖f2	♕xc2!
32	d3	

32 ♗xd5+ ♔h7 33 ♗xd4 ♕d3+

| 32 | ... | ♕b1+! |
| 33 | ♔g2 | c3! |

The bishop is stuck out of play.

34	♗a3	♔g7
35	♗xd5	g5
36	♖f1	♕xd3
37	♗c1	♕e2+!
38	♔g1	♕g4+
39	♔h1	d3
40	♗f3	♕f5
41	♗e3	♕e5
42	♗c5	c2
43	♗xh5	d2
	0 : 1	

The appearance of a new queen is inevitable.

Illustrative game 7
Fischer – Matulovic
Herzeg – Novi
(International Blitz
Tournament) 1970

1	e4	e5
2	♘f3	♘c6
3	♗b5	f5
4	♘c3	fxe4

5	♘xe4	d5
6	♘xe5	dxe4
7	♘xc6	♕g5
8	♕e2	♘f6
9	f4	♕xf4
10	d4	♕h4+
11	g3	♕h3
12	♗g5!	

The strongest continuation. Meeting this variation for the first time, Fischer demonstrates that after 12 ♗g5! Black is struggling to equalise.

12	...	a6
13	♗a4	♗d7
14	♗xf6	gxf6
15	♕xe4+	♔f7

15 ... ♕e6 16 ♕xe6+ ♗xe6 17 0-0!±

Fischer now sacrifices a piece for a strong attack against the enemy king.

16	♘e5+!	fxe5
17	♖f1+	♔e7

17 ... ♔g7? lost at once in view of 18 ♕xe5+ ♔h6 19 ♖f6+ ♔g7 20 ♕g5+

18	♗xd7	♔xd7
19	♖f7+	♔e8

A better chance appears to be 19 ... ♗e7 20 0-0-0 ♔e8. However, after 21 ♖f5! ♖f8 22 ♖xe5 ♖f7 (worse is 22 ... ♕h6+ 23 ♔b1 ♖f7 {23 ... ♕d6 24 ♕xh7} because of 24 ♖e6!) 23 ♖e1 ♕h6+ 24 ♔b1 ♕d6 25 ♕xb7 ♖d8 26 ♕e4 White has a large advantage.

20	♖xc7	♗d6
21	♖xb7	♖c8
22	0-0-0	♕xh2
23	dxe5	♗e7

With three pawns for the piece and an enduring attack, White is winning. The following exchange sacrifice is the quickest way to end the struggle.

24	♖xe7+!	♔xe7
25	♕b7+	♔e6
26	♕d7+	♔xe5
27	♕d5+	♔f6

28	♖f1+	♔g6
29	♕e6+	♔g5
30	♖f5+	♔g4
31	♖f4+	♔xg3
32	♕g4#	

Illustrative game 8
Estrin - Neishtadt
Correspondence 1963/64

1	e4	e5
2	♘f3	♘c6
3	♗b5	f5
4	♘c3	fxe4
5	♘xe4	d5
6	♘xe5	dxe4
7	♘xc6	♕g5
8	♕e2	♘f6
9	f4	♕h4+
10	g3	♕h3
11	♘xa7+	♗d7
12	♗xd7+	♕xd7
13	♘b5	0-0-0

Our earlier analysis shows that 13 ... c6 is not worse for Black.

| 14 | b3 | c6?! |

A questionable move. The best here is 14 ... ♗c5 15 ♗b2 ♘g4∞

15	♘a3!	♕d4
16	c3	♕a7
17	♘c4	

Although Black has some play, the two pawn deficit means that White is for preference.

| 17 | ... | h5 |

| 18 | ♗b2 | h4 |

| 19 | 0-0-0 | |

Best was 19 g4!±

19	...	hxg3
20	hxg3	♖xh1
21	♖xh1	b5

Not 21 ... ♕xa2 22 ♔c2 △ ♖a1.

| 22 | ♘e5 | ♕xa2 |
| 23 | ♘xc6 | |

23 ♔c2 ♗a3 24 ♖b1 ♖h8! △ ... ♖h1

| 23 | ... | ♔c7! |

A very strong and unexpected move. 23 ... ♗a3 would have been answered by 24 ♘a7+! with a winning position

24	♘xd8	♗a3
25	♘e6+	♔d6
26	d3	♕a1+
27	♔d2	♕xb2+
28	♔e3	♕xc3
29	f5	♕e5
30	♔f2!	

White plans to jettison some extra material to regain the initiative.

30	...	♕xf5+
31	♘f4	g5
32	dxe4	♕c5+

After 32 ... ♘xe4+ 33 ♔f3 ♘xg3 White can get a winning position with 34 ♕d2+ ♔c6 35 ♖h6+ ♔b7 36 ♔xg3 gxf4+ 37 ♕xf4

33	♔f3	gxf4
34	gxf4	♕c6
35	♕d3+	♔e7
36	♕d4	♗d6
37	♖a1	♗b8
38	b4	♕e6
39	e5	♕h3+

½ : ½

Illustrative game 9
Kuntselman – Nesterenko
Correspondence 1975/76

1	e4	e5
2	♘f3	♘c6
3	♗b5	f5
4	♘c3	fxe4
5	♘xe4	d5
6	♘xe5	dxe4
7	♘xc6	♕g5
8	♕e2	♘f6
9	f4	♕h4+
10	g3	♕h3
11	♘e5+	c6
12	♗c4	h5!?

The main continuation, as analysed earlier, is 12 ... ♗c5. With the aggressive text, Black intends to launch a fierce attack against the enemy position, involving sacrifices if necessary

13 ♘f7?!

The novelty already begins to take effect. This move allows Black to carry out a bold and unexpected rook sacrifice. Later it was discovered that now is the correct moment to remove the king from the danger zone, e.g. 13 d3! h4 14 ♗e3! hxg3 15 0-0-0! gxh2 (15 ... ♗g4 16 dxe4 ♗h5 17 hxg3 ♕xh1 18 ♖xh1 ♗xe2 19 ♘f7+ ♔d8 20 ♖xh8± Slyuntsevsky – Willem, Holland 1980) 16 dxe4 ♗e7 17 ♕d3± Liberzon – Wockenfuss, Bad Lauterberg 1977.

13 ... h4!

14   ☐g1

Nesterenko's idea has received one further practical test in Hangli - Menne, Oslo 1978: 14 ♘xh8 hxg3 15 ♘g6 (15 ☐g1 leads to the main variation) 15 ... ♗c5 16 d4 ♗xd4 17 ♗e3 ♘g4 18 ♗xd4 and now with 18 ... ♗xe2 19 ♗xe2 ☐d8! Black could play for the advantage

Better than 18 ♗xd4 is 18 ♕d2 when play can continue 18 ... g2! (18 ... ♗xe3 19 ♕xe3 ♗f3 20 ♔d2! {20 ♕c5? 0-0-0 21 ♕e5 ♕g2! 22 ♗e6+ ☐d7 23 ♗xd7+ ♘xd7-+} 20 ... ♗xh1 21 ♕xg3=) 19 ☐g1 ♗xe3 20 ♕xg2 (the tempting 20 ♕d6? loses immediately to 20 ... ♗f2+ 21 ♔xf2 ♕f3+) 20 ... ♗xg1 21 ♕xg1 0-0-0 22 ♕xa7 ♕xh2 23 ♕a8+ ♔c7 24 ♕a5+ with perpetual check.

14   ...   hxg3

15   ♘xh8   gxh2
16   ☐h1   ♗c5
17   ♕xh2

17 ☐xh2 would run into 17 ... ♕g3+ 18 ☐f2 ♗g4 19 ♕f1 ♗h3 20 ♕e2 0-0-0 with decisive threats, e.g. 21 ♘f7 ♘g4 22 ♗e6+ ♔c7 23 ♗xg4 ♗xg4 24 ♕f1 e3!-+

17   ...   ♗f2+!!

A brilliant move regaining material equality and preserving a dangerous initiative.

18   ♕xf2

18 ♔xf2 ♘g4+

18 ♔d1 ♗g4+ 19 ♗e2 ♗xe2+ 20 ♔xe2 ♕f3+ 21 ♔f1 ♗g3+-+

18   ...   ♕xh1+
19   ♗f1   ♕xh8
20   d3   ♗g4
21   ♗e2   0-0-0

Black has succeeded in regaining the sacrificed material and now has a winning initiative.

22   ♗d2   ☐e8

23	♗xg4+	♘xg4
24	♕g1	♕h4+
25	♔e2	

25 ♔d1 ♘f2+ 26 ♔c1 e3 27 ♗e1 ♕xf4–+

25	...	exd3+
	0 : 1	

A splendid game.

Illustrative game 10
Heemsoth –
Konstantinopolsky
Vidmar Memorial
Correspondence
Tournament 1976/78

1	e4	e5
2	♘f3	♘c6
3	♗b5	f5
4	♘c3	fxe4
5	♘xe4	d5
6	♘xe5	dxe4
7	♘xc6	♕g5
8	♕e2	♘f6
9	f4	♕h4+
10	g3	♕h3
11	♘e5+	c6
12	♗c4	♗c5
13	d3	♘g4
14	♕xe4	♘f2
15	♗f7+	

For 15 ♕e2 see the theoretical section.

see following diagram

15	...	♔d8

15 ... ♔e7 can lead to the

15	...	♔d8

15 ... ♔e7 can lead to the following play: 16 ♕c4 ♗b6 17 ♖f1 ♕xh2! 18 ♕b4+ (18 ♗g8 ♕xg3!; 18 ♗d2 ♕xg3!) 18 ... c5 19 ♕d2 ♘g4 20 ♕xh2 ♘xh2 21 ♖h1 ♘g4 22 ♘xg4 ♔xf7 23 ♘e5+ ♔f6 and although White has an extra pawn, Black has good chances for the draw.

16	♕c4	♗b6
17	♖f1	

Black clearly has serious difficulties and it is not easy for him to find a satisfactory defence.

17   ...   ♘g4

The correspondence game Konikowski – Ross, 1977 saw 17 ... ♕xh2 18 ♕b4 ♔c7 (18 ... c5 would be met by 19 ♕d2 ♘g4 20 ♕xh2 ♘xh2 21 ♖h1 ♘g4 22 ♘g6!+–) 19 ♗e3! ♘g4 (of course not 19 ... ♗xe3? 20 ♕e7+) 20 ♗xb6+ axb6 21 ♕e7+ ♔b8 22 ♕d6+! (not 22 0-0-0 when 22 ... ♖a5! equalises the chances) 22 ...♔a7 23 0-0-0 ♕xg3 24

♘xg4 ♗xg4 25 ♖de1±

The text move doesn't save Black either.

18   ♘xg4   ♕xg4
19   f5!   ♕xc4

19 ... ♗xf5 20 ♖f4 ♕h3 21 ♖h4 ♕g2 22 ♗g5+ ♔d7 23 0-0-0 with an easily winning position for White.

20   ♗g5+   ♔c7
21   ♗xc4

... and with two extra pawns, White won easily.

1 : 0

Index of Variations